# Acknowledgements

CW01501439

Warm thanks are due to the colleagues who have helped bring this book to fruition including Nicolas Bell, Marc Gotthardt, Anne McLaughlin, Bill O'Hearn, Anne Toner, Fernanda Valencia, and Paula Wolff. I am particularly indebted to Nicolas Bell, the Librarian, for his assistance with the illustrations, and to Alessandra Tosi at Open Book Publishers, for the alacrity with which she welcomed the proposal. And special gratitude is owing to David Manns, Trinity alumnus, whose generous donation has made this publication possible.

For permission to reprint the chapters that make up this volume, we are grateful to the following: the executors of Anne Barton's Estate for 'Lord Byron and Trinity: a bicentenary portrait', *Trinity Review* (1988); Liverpool University Press for Robert Beevers, 'Pretensions to Permanency: Thorvaldsen's Bust and Statue of Byron', *Byron Journal* (January 1995); David St Clair for William St Clair, 'Poets and Travellers', Ch. 17 in *Lord Elgin and the Marbles: the controversial history of the Parthenon Sculptures*, 3rd revised edition (Oxford and New York: Oxford University Press, 1998); and the Universidad Nacional Autónoma de México for Adrian Poole, an earlier version of whose text was published under the title 'Byron in Yucatán: War and Ruins', in *The Influence and Legacy of Alexander von Humboldt in the Americas*, edited by María Fernanda Valencia Suárez and Carolina Depetris (Merida: UNAM, 2022).

# About the Contributors

**Anne Barton** (1933–2013) was an eminent Shakespeare scholar and literary critic. Her most celebrated book *Shakespeare and the Idea of the Play*, adapted from her doctoral thesis at Girton College, Cambridge and published in 1962 under her former name Anne Righter, looked at Shakespeare's historical and theatrical context to examine his relationship with plays, actors, and the audience. Some of her other publications include *Ben Jonson, Dramatist* (1982), *The Names of Comedy* (1990), and *Byron: Don Juan* (1992). Barton was a distinguished academic, holding positions as a Professor of English at Cambridge University and Fellow of Trinity College. She was also the first woman fellow at New College, Oxford where she taught for ten years. In 1991, she was elected a Fellow of the British Academy.

**Robert Beevers** (1919–2010) was elected Director of Regional Tutorial Services at the Open University (OU) at its establishment in 1969. As one of the university's 'founding fathers', Beevers played a critical role in creating the university's tutor and counsellor system as well as the regional study centres that function outside of its headquarters at Milton Keynes. Beyond his work at the OU, Beevers wrote a biography of British urban planner and social reformer Ebenezer Howard entitled *The Garden City Utopia* (1988). In retirement, Beevers published *The Byronic Image: The Poet Portrayed* (2005), which analyses portraits of the poet.

**Charles Tennyson Turner** (1808–1879) was an English poet and elder brother of Alfred Lord Tennyson. The two attended Trinity College, Cambridge together. After graduating, Turner pursued a life in the church—acting as the vicar of Grasby, Lincolnshire from 1836 until his death. Influenced by Byron at an early age, Turner published a considerable body of poems, writing a total of 350 sonnets over the course of his life. Some of his more notable publications include *Sonnets, Lyrics and Translations* (1873) and, co-authored book with his brother, *Poems by Two Brothers* (1827).

**William St Clair** (1937–2021) worked as a civil servant in the Treasury for many years before proceeding to Fellowships at All Souls, Oxford, then Trinity College, Cambridge, and finally the Institute of English Studies at the School of Advanced Study, University of London. His passion for history motivated him to publish *Lord Elgin and the Marbles* in 1967, a pioneering study of the controversial acquisition of the Parthenon Marbles. In the book's third edition (1998), St Clair exposed how attempts to whiten the Greek relics by the British Museum led to their damage. Equally invested in the world of literature, St Clair published books and articles on the genre of British biography, on writers of the Romantic period, most notably Byron, and in his massive study, *The Reading Nation*, on the history of books. He was elected a Fellow of the British Academy in 1992. His belief in open-access publishing led him to co-found Open Book Publishers in 2008; he acted as its Chairman until his death.

**Adrian Poole** (1948– ) is an Emeritus Professor of English Literature at Cambridge University and Fellow of Trinity College. His research interests include comparative tragedy, prose fiction, and the impact of Shakespeare on English literature. In 2022, he won the Modern Language Association Prize for his scholarly edition of Henry James's novel *The Princess Casamassima*, part of *The Cambridge Edition of the Complete Fiction of Henry James.*

# BYRON AND TRINITY

# Byron and Trinity

## Memorials, Marbles and Ruins

*Edited by Adrian Poole*

OpenBook Publishers

ISBN Paperback: 978-1-80511-278-5
ISBN Hardback: 978-1-80511-279-2
ISBN Digital (PDF): 978-1-80064-280-8
ISBN Digital eBook (EPUB): 978-1-80511-281-5
ISBN Digital (HTML): 978-1-80511-283-9

DOI: 10.11647/OBP.0399

Cover photo: Statue of Lord Byron by the Danish sculptor Bertel Thorvaldsen. Photograph by James Kirwan, courtesy of the Master and Fellows of Trinity College, Cambridge.
Cover design by Jeevanjot Kaur Nagpal

# Contents

# List of Illustrations

Fig. 0.1   Anne Barton's memorial brass in the Trinity College Ante-chapel. Photograph by Adrian Poole.

Fig. 1.1 *The statue of Sir Isaac Newton in the Trinity College Ante-Chapel*, by Louis-François Roubiliac (1755). Photograph by Adrian Poole.

Fig. 1.2   The memorial bust of Thomas Jones, Byron's tutor, in the Trinity College Ante-Chapel, by Joseph Nollekens (n.d.). Photograph by Joanna Harries, courtesy of the Master and Fellows of Trinity College, Cambridge.

Fig. 2.1 Bertel Thorvaldsen, *George Gordon Byron*, original plaster model of the bust of Byron (April–May 1817). Thorvaldsens Museum, photograph by Jakob Faurvig, CC0, https://kataloget.thorvaldsensmuseum.dk/en/A257.

Fig. 2.2   Bertel Thorvaldsen, *George Gordon Byron*, marble bust of Byron (1824). Thorvaldsens Museum, photograph by Jakob Faurvig, CC0, https://kataloget.thorvaldsensmuseum.dk/en/A256.

Fig. 2.3   Bertel Thorvaldsen, *Monument for George Gordon Byron*, pencil sketch of Byron statue (1830). Thorvaldsens Museum, photograph by Helle Nanny Brendstrup, CC0, https://kataloget.thorvaldsensmuseum.dk/en/C352.

Fig. 2.4   Bertel Thorvaldsen, *Monument for George Gordon Byron with the Relief the Genius of Poetry on the Plinth*, pencil sketch of Byron statue and relief for the plinth (1830–31). Thorvaldsens Museum, photograph by Jakob Faurvig, CC0, https://kataloget.thorvaldsensmuseum.dk/en/C350r.

Fig. 2.5  Bertel Thorvaldsen, *Monument to George Gordon Byron*, full-size plaster model of statue of Byron (May 1831). Thorvaldsens Museum, photograph by Jakob Faurvig, CC0, https://kataloget. thorvaldsensmuseum.dk/en/A130.

Fig. 2.6 Bertel Thorvaldsen, statue of Byron in the Wren Library, showing the owl of Minerva and the skull as memento mori. Courtesy of Trinity College, Cambridge.

Fig. 2.7  Photograph of the Byron statue shortly after its installation in the Wren Library in 1845. Courtesy of Trinity College, Cambridge (Add. PG.13[5]).

Fig. 5.1  Adrian Poole and other tourists at Cobá, Mexico, November 2018. Photograph by Margaret de Vaux.

# Foreword

## *Adrian Poole*

This collection of essays reprints some writings about Lord Byron, the most celebrated writer to have passed through Trinity College, Cambridge, for the bi-centennial commemoration of his death on 19 April 1824. It also contains a full bibliography of primary and secondary sources cited. Links to openly available primary resources, wherever available, have been added to the references for ease of access.

Three of the essays are by Fellows of the College: Anne Barton (1933–2013), who wrote a commemorative piece for *The Trinity Review* on the bicentenary of Byron's birth in 1988;[1] William St Clair (1937–2021), whose chapter on 'Poets and Travellers' in his book on *Lord Elgin and the Marbles* (3rd revised edition, 1998) is centred on Byron; and Adrian Poole (1948– ), whose essay on Byron and John Lloyd Stephens, the American traveller credited with the 'discovery' of the Mayan ruins in Central America, reflects on the legacy of the poet's preoccupation with ruins. The fourth is by Robert Beevers (1919–2010), who describes the process by which the great statue of Byron by the Danish sculptor, Bertel Thorvaldsen, ended up in the Wren Library. Associated with this is the sonnet 'On the Statue of Lord Byron', written by Charles Tennyson Turner (1808–1879), elder brother of the more famous Lord Alfred.

The volume's sub-title makes a certain claim for its coherence in the relations between 'memorials', 'marbles' and 'ruins', in so far as these subjects entail a continuity essential to Byron's own thinking and feeling.

---

1 Anne herself has a commemorative plaque in the Ante-Chapel (see Fig. 0.1), that notes her eminence as a critic not only of Shakespeare and Jonson, especially their comedies, but also the poetry of 'our own Byron': OPERA SHAKESPEARIANA ET JONSONIANA PRAESERTIM COMICA NECNON BYRONIS NOSTRI CARMINA

    https://doi.org/10.11647/OBP.0399.00

Important scholarly and critical work has been done on these aspects of his life and writing, including his life-*in*-writing, much of it post-dating the essays reprinted here.[2] Nevertheless the present collection represents a modest means of honouring a figure of enduring, complex significance, of whose association with Trinity the College is proud. Given the large margin by which Byron failed to be a model student, he would have been astonished.

Not for the first time: Anne Barton recalls the ovation with which the author of *Childe Harold* was greeted by Cambridge students at the Senate House in 1814. But to borrow a famous saying from Shakespeare, while 'the whirligig of time brings in his revenges',[3] it also prompts reflection on all the other challenges and opportunities with which it is freighted. It makes us consider how many words we need that begin with the prefix 're-', including remembrance, reconciliation, reparation, restoration, renovation. And how complex it may be to make them real. Which is one reason, among many, why we still need to read Byron.

Fig 0.1 Anne Barton's memorial brass in the Trinity College Ante-chapel. Photograph by Adrian Poole.

---

2    On the visual commemoration of Byron, for example, see Geoffrey Bond and Christine Kenyon Jones, *Dangerous to Show: Byron and His Portraits* (London: Unicorn, 2020), pp. 76–84, which includes some valuable commentary on the Thorvaldsen statue, and some details not included in Beevers's article.

3    Feste's words in *Twelfth Night*, Act 5, scene 1.

# 1. Lord Byron and Trinity

## A Bicentenary Portrait[1]

### *Anne Barton*

When this year's Clark Lecturer,[2] Jerome McCann, slyly called Lord Byron 'Trinity's most adorable pet', a frisson of uncertainty rippled through the audience at Mill Lane. Suddenly, two possible meanings of the adjective 'adorable' were in collision: 'worthy of reverence and honour', the original sense, forced up against the more modern signification 'charming, personally lovable and attractive'. For a moment, everyone in the room appeared to be trying to decide in which sense Byron might be adorable—or was it neither, or both? With no other Trinity poet, whether Marvell, Cowley, Dryden, Tennyson, or any of the rest, could such a dilemma arise. Assessments of Byron, on the other hand, in this bicentenary year of his birth, remain both contradictory and oddly personal and intense, as though this man had died only recently, rather than one hundred and sixty-four years ago. Nor has it proved possible to divorce the life and personality from the work.

For the young Byron's long-suffering tutors at Trinity, the case was rather different. What they had on their hands for three scattered University terms, beginning in Michaelmas 1805, must have seemed in no sense 'adorable': a moody, extravagant, high-handed young man bitterly disappointed to be at Cambridge rather than Oxford with most

---

1   Published in *The Trinity Review* (1988) for the bicentenary of Byron's birth. Reprinted by permission of the Executors of Anne Barton's Estate.
2   These lectures, normally annual, were established in 1878 from a bequest of William George Clark; they are typically, though not exclusively, addressed to topics in English literature.

   https://doi.org/10.11647/OBP.0399.01

of his Harrow friends. He was temporarily consoled by finding himself the possessor of '*super*excellent rooms'[3] (probably, as Robert Robson has suggested, I1 Nevile's Court),[4] where freed from the surveillance of a devoted but exasperating mother, he could begin to run himself seriously into debt. He also fell in love ('a violent, though *pure* love and passion')[5] with one of the choirboys in the chapel. The Christmas vacation took Byron to London and there, despite remonstrances from Trinity, not to mention the threat of disciplinary action from the Court of the Chancery, of which he was a ward, he lingered for months, returning to Cambridge only in the summer term. He brought back with him an enlarged acquaintance with London bawds, and also with professional boxers, jockeys and fencing masters, low tastes for which his tutor Thomas Jones unavailingly reproached him. He would be engaged, before long, in an altercation with the Mayor of Cambridge, who took a dim view of Byron's proposal to establish his fencing-master permanently in the town.

At the end of term, Byron vanished again, this time for a year. His fine rooms, re-allocated to Charles Skinner Matthews, another undergraduate, were still overflowing with Byron's belongings and the Senior Tutor felt obliged to issue a nervous caution to the new occupant, 'for Lord Byron, Sir, is a young man of *tumultuous passions*'.[6] When the ogre re-appeared, however, late in June 1807, to remove them, having announced his intention of abandoning Trinity for good, he made no complaint but after renewing acquaintance with old friends, and making several new ones—including Matthews himself—decided abruptly to give Cambridge another try. Byron was now nineteen. During his year of truancy, the

3    Letter to Augusta Byron, 6 November 1805, in *Byron's Letters and Journals*, ed. by Leslie A. Marchand, 13 vols (London: John Murray, 1973–94), I, 79. All subsequent references to Byron's *Letters and Journals* are to this edition, hereafter *BLJ*.

4    Robert Robson, 'Byron's rooms revisited', *The Trinity Review* (Easter 1975), 22–24. Robson supports the probable veracity of J. W. Clark's statement in *Cambridge, Historical and Descriptive Notes* (1890), p. 138, about the location of Byron's room in I1 Nevile's Court, Trinity College, Cambridge, and the high improbability of the legend, derived from M. F. Wright's *Alma Mater, or Seven Years at the University of Cambridge, by a Trinity-Man* (1827), that Byron and his bear were lodged in the south-east corner of the Great Court, K staircase. About the situation of the bear, Robson cites Clark's statement that it was kept 'in a stable in the Ram Yard', noting that 'it is highly improbable to say the least that the College authorities would then have tolerated a bear in the College', and even more drily that 'it is unlikely even now, when discipline is a good deal less stringent than it was' (22).

5    *Ravenna Journal*, 12 January 1821; *BLJ* VIII, 22.

6    Letter to John Murray, 18 November 1820; *BLJ* VII, 232.

fat, idle, relatively unsophisticated youth the college remembered had been transformed. He had been in and out of a great many beds, had just published a collection of poems and, although there was nothing he could do about his congenital lameness, the purposeful shedding of several stone in weight had released from captivity a slim young man of arresting physical beauty. Just in case he might fail, nonetheless, to attract attention, Byron came back into residence for the Michaelmas term 1807 accompanied by a tame bear. Trinity's statutes had long prohibited undergraduates from bringing their dogs into college, but the imagination of the authorities had not encompassed the need to fend off bears.

Byron's reply to urgent tutorial enquiries about what he meant to do with the beast was that 'he should *sit* for *a Fellowship*'.[7] (He was later to pretend, in the postscript to the second edition of *English Bards and Scotch Reviewers*, that only 'the jealousy of his Trinity contemporaries prevented him from success'.)[8] It was a joke with a cutting edge. Although Byron's tutor Jones had successfully pressed, some years before, for fellowship elections to be conducted openly rather than in private, they were still susceptible to charges of favouritism and abuse. As a nobleman, moreover, Byron regularly dined in Hall with the fellows of Trinity. His impression of them as a group he had communicated earlier in letters written from Cambridge: 'Study is the last pursuit of the society; the Master eats, drinks, and sleeps, the fellows *drink, dispute*, and *pun*'. Their pursuits, he claimed, were 'limited to the Church,—not of Christ, but of the nearest benefice'.[9] In 'Thoughts Suggested by a College Examination', a satirical poem published in his collection of 1807, *Hours of Idleness*, he made his contempt more public:

> The sons of science, these, who thus repaid,
> Linger in ease, in Granta's sluggish shade;
> Where on Cam's sedgy banks supine they lie,
> Unknown, unhonour'd live,—unwept for, die;
> Dull as the pictures, which adorn their halls,
> They think all learning fix'd within their walls;
> In manners rude, in foolish forms precise,

---

7    Letter to Elizabeth Bridget Pigot, 26 October 1807; *BLJ* I, 135–36.

8    *English Bards, and Scotch Reviewers: A Satire*, 2ⁿᵈ edn (London, 1809). Reprinted in https://petercochran.files.wordpress.com/2009/03/english-bards-and-scotch-reviewers1.pdf

9    Letters to John Hanson, 23 November 1805, and Robert Charles Dallas, 21 January 1808; *BLJ* I, 81, 147.

All modern arts, affecting to despise;
Yet prizing Bentley's, Brunck's, or Porson's note,
More than the verses, on which the critic wrote;
Vain as their honours, heavy as their Ale,
Sad as their wit, and tedious as their tale,
To friendship dead, though not untaught to feel,
When Self and Church demand a Bigot zeal. [...]
Such are the men, who learning's treasures guard,
Such is their practice, such is their reward;
This much, at least, we may presume to say;
The premium can't exceed the price they pay.[10]

If, as Hobhouse later asserted,[11] Byron was indeed the undergraduate that the great classical scholar Porson, Regius Professor of Greek at Trinity, once tried to assault with a poker, the attack was not entirely unprovoked.

When Byron included 'Thoughts Suggested' in the first edition of *Hours of Idleness*, he believed he had finished with Cambridge forever. He was a little nervous about the poem, all the same, especially after his own unexpected return to 'Granta's sluggish shade'. On the 20 November 1807, he wrote from Trinity instructing his publisher Ridge to omit it from the second edition. But, by 14 December, as term drew to a close, he had changed his mind, not only countermanding the November deletion, but adding four new lines, those beginning 'Vain are their honours...' to the original. It was one of the first examples of what was to become Byron's characteristic reluctance to let go of a poem even after it had been published, the urgent need to carry forward with his own life what he had written months, or even years, before. In this instance, the accretion signalled another decision, this time irrevocable, to abandon Cambridge. Between Christmas 1807 and the spring of 1816, when he was (or felt himself) driven from England by the scandal surrounding the break-up of his marriage, Byron would return several times to visit or offer support to friends. His official connection with the University came to an end, however, in July 1808, when he finally took that MA which Cambridge, in his case, was most reluctant to award.

---

10   *Byron: The Complete Poetical Works*, ed. by Jerome J. McGann, 7 vols (Oxford: Clarendon Press, 1980–93), I, 94. All subsequent references to Byron's poetry are to this edition, hereafter *CPW*.

11   Peter Cochran, *Byron and Hobby-O: Lord Byron's Relationship with John Cam Hobhouse* (Newcastle-upon-Tyne: Cambridge Scholars Publishing, 2010), p. 313.

'The university still chew the Cud of my degree', he informed his friend Hobhouse (who was still at Trinity) in March of that year: 'please God they shall swallow it, though Inflammation be the Consequence.'[12]

Ironically Byron owed his MA to precisely that academic venality and corruption about which he was so scathing both in letters of the period and in his satirical Cambridge poems. It was his bare three terms of residence which made the degree problematic, not the fact that he had never taken an examination nor, so far as is known, bothered to attend lectures. In 1787, Byron's tutor Thomas Jones had made the radical proposal that noblemen and wealthy fellow-commoners should be obliged to take examinations just like financially dependent undergraduates, the pensioners and sizars. The Grace was defeated in the Senate House. Like other peers, Byron received his degree in exchange for going through a few minutes of whispered 'disputation' with his tutor in the Senate House, and handing the latter, (no longer, at least, Jones) a fat fee.

That Jones, before his death in July 1807, had occasionally remonstrated with his noble pupil on academic grounds, not simply because of his absences and animals, is clear from the defensive letter Byron addressed to him early in 1807. 'I have adopted a distinct line of Reading', Byron asserted, in the course of explaining why he had declined to avail himself of the formal instruction offered in mathematics, theology and philosophy: 'this you will probably *smile* at, & imagine (as you *very* naturally may) that because I have not pursued my College Studies, I have pursued *none*.—I have certainly no right to be offended at such a Conjecture, nor indeed am I, that it is erroneous, Time will perhaps discover'.[13] Time has not, in fact, revealed any coherent programme of study equivalent to the one Wordsworth (another defector from the Cambridge syllabus) had devised for himself in Modern Languages during his time at St John's. It seems clear, however, that the Byron who had complained in his first term of residence that 'nobody here seems to look into an author ancient or modern if they can avoid it',[14] did in fact continue to read avidly, if without system, at Cambridge, as indeed throughout his life. The grounds of his classical education had been laid before he came up to Trinity. Most of the translations from Greek and

---

12   Letter to John Cam Hobhouse, 26 March 1808; *BLJ* I, 161.
13   Letter to Rev. Thomas Jones, 14 February 1807; *BLJ* I, 108.
14   Letter to Hargreaves Hanson, 12 November 1805; *BLJ* I, 80.

Latin published in his first volume of poems were products of the Harrow years. History he had always loved. It seems, however, to have been at Cambridge that English literature and, in particular, contemporary poetry, began to engage him seriously. They played, of course, no part in his official studies. Indeed, one of Byron's chief complaints in 'Thoughts Suggested' was the ignorance of English history, law and literature fostered by the University syllabus:

> Happy the youth! in Euclid's axioms tried,
> Though little vers'd in any art beside;
> Who, scarcely skill'd an English line to pen,
> Scans Attic metres with a critic's ken.
> What ! though he knows not how his fathers bled,
> When civil discord pil'd the fields with dead;
> When Edward bade his conquering bands advance,
> Or Henry trampled on the crests of France;
> Though, marv'lling at the name of Magna Carta,
> Yet, well he recollects the laws of Sparta;
> Can tell what edicts sage Lycurgus made,
> Whilst Blackstone's on the shelf, neglected, laid;
> Of Grecian dramas vaunts the deathless fame,
> Of Avon's bard, rememb'ring scarce the name.[15]

During his last term at Trinity, Byron completed 'above four hundred lines' of verse anatomizing 'the poetry of the present Day'.[16] 'British Bards: A Satire', its initial title, was a youthful polemic which, in lengthening versions, was to go through five editions. Byron came to wish he had never published it at all. Although his faith in Milton, Dryden and Pope as standards of excellence remained fixed, he was later embarrassed by many of the judgements passed on his contemporaries. This poem written in part at Trinity is important, however, because without amounting to the kind of self-dedication Wordsworth had vowed in the summer vacation of his first year at Cambridge, it nonetheless signalled a commitment to poetry, his own and that of other people, about which Byron would often become impatient in the future, even somewhat ashamed, but which was to remain with him for the rest of his life. The Cambridge he knew may have seemed 'a villainous Chaos of Dice and Drunkenness, nothing but Hazard and Burgundy, Hunting,

---

15   *CPW* I, 92–93.
16   Letter to Ben Crosby, 22 December 1807; *BLJ* I, 141.

Mathematics and Newmarket, Riot and Racing' as he described it in a letter written during that final term.[17] Byron's life there had not been spent in simple acquiescence to its fashionable *'Monotony of endless variety'.*[18]

The Byron who, several years later,[19] was given a spontaneous ovation by the undergraduates, and honoured by the dons when he entered the Senate House to vote in a University election had become, doubtless to the astonishment of most of the members of Trinity's High Table, a famous man: the author of *Childe Harold, The Giaour, The Bride of Abydos, Lara* and *The Corsair.* The impact of these romantic poems on the reading public, compounded as it was by the personal magnetism of their author, had been virtually without precedent. Works immediately inspired by the travels in Turkey, Greece and Albania on which Byron embarked after taking his MA, and by his perennial need to find objectifying fictional forms for his own emotional entanglements (which by now included a dangerous liaison with Augusta Leigh, his married half-sister), there was little in their conscious exoticism that seemed to link them to his University days. Yet like Wordsworth, Byron had been influenced to a greater and more permanent extent than he recognised by attitudes and ideas which he encountered in the Cambridge of his time.

On 21 January 1808, a month after his final departure from the University, Byron wrote a letter to Robert Charles Dallas, shortly to become his literary agent, in which he provided 'a brief compendium of the Sentiments of the *wicked* George Ld. B'. They included the belief that virtue was *'a feeling* not a principle', the conviction that human actions were governed by the privileging of pleasure over pain (the last, he joked, borne in upon him after getting the worst of an argument, tellingly conjoined with a fall from his horse), that 'Truth was the prime attribute of the Deity,' and death 'an eternal Sleep'. He also claimed to prefer Confucius to the ten commandments, and Socrates to St Paul, to be sceptical about Holy Communion, and, while disallowing any acknowledgment of the Pope, to favour Catholic emancipation in

---

17    Letter to Elizabeth Bridget Pigot, 26 October 1807; *BLJ* I, 135.

18    Letter to Elizabeth Bridget Pigot, 5 July 1807; *BLJ* I, 125.

19    Late October 1814. *Memoir of the Rev. Francis Hodgson, B.D., scholar, poet, and divine: with numerous letters from Lord Byron and others, by his son, James T. Hodgson,* 2 vols (London: Macmillan, 1878), I, 292, https://www.digitale-sammlungen.de/en/view/bsb11370276?page=346,347

England.[20] As a collection of issues and opinions, it was a distinctively Cambridge blend.

Unlike Oxford at the equivalent moment of time, Byron's Cambridge had been profoundly marked by the presence and work of Isaac Newton. The legacy of Newton was visible not only in the emphasis on mathematics in the Tripos, but in tendencies towards free-thinking and scepticism which impelled many members of the university into deism and a few others (like Byron's friend Charles Matthews) into openly confessed atheism. In the realm of moral philosophy, the mechanistic implications of Newton's thought encouraged a belief in the pleasure principle as the foundation of human action, and in materialist, utilitarian goals. In this climate, the ancient statute debarring anyone who refused to subscribe to the Thirty-nine Articles of the Church of England from taking a degree began to seem oppressive: there was pressure to withdraw it, allowing Unitarians and members of dissenting religions, including Catholics, the same rights as Anglicans. Politically, too, as well as in matters of religion, Cambridge in the late eighteenth and early nineteenth century harboured a good deal of radicalism. The effort by Byron's tutor Jones to subject all undergraduates, regardless of wealth or rank, to the same academic requirements, although defeated at the time, was symptomatic of a democratizing impulse which extended to far wider, non-university issues of political and social reform. Nowhere in Cambridge were these liberal tendencies more pronounced than at Trinity, Newton's own former college.

At Harrow, Byron's close friends had almost all been noblemen like himself. At Cambridge they were not. In his final term he became a member of the Cambridge Whig Club and for the rest of his life remained fiercely anti-Tory. Of Byron's three speeches in Parliament, delivered shortly after he had left Cambridge, one was a plea for Catholic emancipation, another a protest against the use of the death penalty to quell industrial unrest among the Nottingham cloth workers, while the third defended a parliamentary informer. Later on, he was to become deeply involved in the abortive Italian revolution and finally, when social ferment in England disappointingly failed to result in action, to die in the Greek War of Independence. Before then, he had written sixteen Cantos of *Don Juan*, his unfinished masterpiece, in which

---

20    Letter to Robert Charles Dallas, 21 January 1808; *BLJ* I, 148.

the radicalism and scepticism to which he had first been attracted at Cambridge found their mature poetic expression.

Unlike the early Cantos of *Childe Harold*, *Don Juan* was not a success with the reading public. Indeed, it came in for increasing moral castigation and abuse, even John Murray, Byron's publisher for many years, finally declining to handle material so dangerously brilliant.

> They accuse me—*Me*—the present writer of
> The present poem of—I know not what,—
> A tendency to under-rate and scoff
> At human power and virtue and all that;
> And this they say in language rather rough.
> Good God! I wonder what they would be at![21]

Caught in his last years, artistically as well as personally by one of England's fiercest relapses into puritanism and orthodoxy, Byron nevertheless pressed on, in his Italian exile, with a 'shocking' poem that no one (except Shelley) prized. In Ravenna, from a distance of some fourteen years, his time at Cambridge—the days of swimming in 'Cam's [...] not [...] very "translucent" wave', the reading, the conviviality and good talk—suddenly came back to him as 'the happiest, perhaps, days of my life'.[22] John Cam Hobhouse, Byron's Trinity contemporary, had remained a close if misguidedly loyal friend. After Byron's death, he nervously burnt the poet's manuscript *Memoirs*, in order to safeguard his 'reputation'. He would have liked to 'lose' *Don Juan* too.

That poem has effectively had to wait until the twentieth century to find its public, to be seen for what Byron, as he went on writing it, gradually realised that it was: in its unorthodox way, a genuinely moral work. Infinitely inventive, both funny and sad, it interweaves Byron's idiosyncratic version of the Don Juan story with the record of an individual life—his own—lived so expansively and on so many different levels that an entire epoch of European history seems contained within it. Significantly, it is a poem haunted by the figure of Newton, the man whose discoveries had dominated the Cambridge of Byron's youth. For Blake and for Keats, Newton figured as imagination's enemy. Wordsworth, although influenced like Byron by Newtonian ideas, put the man himself into his autobiographical poem, *The Prelude*, only as an

---

21  *Don Juan*, Canto VII, 3; *CPW* V, 337
22  *Ravenna Journal*, 12 January 1821; *BLJ* VIII, 24, 23.

afterthought: a memory of the statue in Trinity chapel, with its 'prism and silent face, / The marble index of a mind forever / Voyaging through strange seas of Thought, alone'.[23] Byron, more complexly, saw Newton as a kind of Janus figure, embodying on the one hand the immeasurable capabilities of the human mind:

> When Newton saw an apple fall, he found
> In that slight startle from his contemplation—
> 'Tis *said* (for I'll not answer above ground
> For any sage's creed or calculation)—
> A mode of proving that the earth turned round
> In a most natural whirl called 'Gravitation,'
> And this is the sole mortal who could grapple,
> Since Adam, with a fall, or with an apple.
>
> Man fell with apples, and with apples rose,
> If this be true, for we must deem the mode
> In which Sir Isaac Newton could disclose
> Through the then unpaved stars the turnpike road,
> A thing to counterbalance human woes;[24]

But he was also obsessed by Newton's own wry description, shortly before his death, of himself as merely 'a boy playing on the sea-shore, and diverting myself in now and then finding a smoother pebble or a prettier shell than ordinary, whilst the great ocean of truth lay undiscovered before me'.[25]

Between these two views of man's potentialities and achievement, one optimistic, the other despairing, Byron's epic vacillates and swings. When the narrator writes of his recoil from 'the abyss of thought', in favour of 'a calm and shallow station / Well nigh the shore, where one stoops down and gathers / Some pretty shell',[26] the aged Newton, through some strange act of ventriloquism, authorises Byron's own characteristic distrust of metaphysical and religious systems. But Byron is also invoking Newton when, immediately after the stanzas about the apple's fall, he defiantly characterises *Don Juan* itself—that unsparing investigation of human social, sexual and political relationships—as a voyage into the

---

23    William Wordsworth, *The Prelude* (London: Moxon, 1850), Book III, lines 60–63.

24    *Don Juan*, Canto X, 1, 2; *CPW* V, 437.

25    Words supposedly uttered by Newton shortly before his death in 1727, reported by Joseph Spence in *Anecdotes, Observations and Characters, of Books and Men* (1820), I, 158; referred to in *Don Juan*, Canto VII, 5; *CPW* V, 338.

26    *Don Juan*, Canto IX, 18; *CPW* V, 414.

unknown equivalent to those undertaken by scientists, men 'who by the dint of glass and vapour / Discover stars and sail in the wind's eye'.[27]

After Byron's death in Greece, at the age of thirty-six, his friend Hobhouse's request that he be buried in 'Poet's Corner' of Westminster Abbey was firmly refused.[28] The Abbey also declined a few years later to accept the life-size statue of Byron by the Danish sculptor Thorvaldsen. Trinity, to whom the piece was finally offered, after it had languished for nine years in the Customs House, proved more courageous. The figure of Byron, seated on a broken Greek column, dominates the long sweep of the Wren Library much as the image of Newton dominates Trinity's Ante-Chapel (see Fig. 1.1). And the man it represents still arouses passionate reactions of love and hate. Only last year [1987], at a conference in Venice, the former Labour leader Michael Foot came close to assaulting an opponent who maintained that Byron was not, after all, a hero of the socialist movement. T. S. Eliot visited upon the face sculpted by Thorvaldsen an intensely personal dislike: 'that weakly sensual mouth, that restless triviality of expression, and worst of all that blind look of the self-conscious beauty'.[29] Those, on the other hand, for whom Byron's elusive but compelling personality continues to speak by way of the richest and most brilliant collection of letters in the language, and also in one of its greatest long poems, read that face rather differently. It seems, in any case, wholly appropriate that the author of *Don Juan* should be commemorated by a statue in the Wren Library rather than in the Abbey. That poem was, in a sense, begun in Cambridge, the place where Byron became confirmed in his adherence to two principles which, as he later said, were the only constant features of his mercurial life and work: the 'strong love of liberty, and a detestation of cant'.[30]

---

27   *Don Juan*, Canto X, 3; *CPW* V, 437.

28   [ed.: Geoffrey Bond and Christine Kenyon Jones recall Thomas Babington Macaulay's observation that 'we know no spectacle so ridiculous as the British public in one of its periodical fits of morality', quoted in *Dangerous to Show: Byron and His Portraits* (London: Unicorn, 2020), p. 81. Unlike Byron, Macaulay does enjoy a memorial statue in Trinity's Ante-chapel. There is also a memorial bust of Byron's tutor, Rev. Thomas Jones (see Fig. 1.2), 'per viginti annos Tutor eximius' ('for twenty years an outstanding Tutor').]

29   *The Complete Prose of T. S. Eliot: The Critical Edition, Volume 5: Tradition and Orthodoxy, 1934–1939*, ed. by Iman Javadi and Ronald Schuchard and Jayme Stayer (Baltimore, MA, and London: The Johns Hopkins University Press and Faber & Faber Ltd., 2017), p. 431.

30   *Conversations of Lord Byron with the Countess of Blessington* (London: H. Colburn, 1834), p. 390, https://babel.hathitrust.org/cgi/pt?id=dul1.ark:/13960/t2795c725&seq=13

Fig. 1.1. The statue of Sir Isaac Newton in the Trinity College Ante-Chapel, by Louis-François Roubiliac (1755). Photograph by Adrian Poole.

Fig. 1.2 The memorial bust of Thomas Jones, Byron's tutor, in the Trinity College Ante-Chapel, by Joseph Nollekens (n.d.). Photograph by Joanna Harries, courtesy of the Master and Fellows of Trinity College, Cambridge.

# 2. Pretensions to Permanency

## Thorvaldsen's Bust and Statue of Byron[1]

### *Robert Beevers*

Fig. 2.1 Bertel Thorvaldsen, *George Gordon Byron*, original plaster model of the bust of Byron (April–May 1817). Thorvaldsens Museum, photograph by Jakob Faurvig, CC0, https://kataloget.thorvaldsensmuseum.dk/en/A257.

---

1    Published in *The Byron Journal*, 23 (Jan. 1995), 63–75. Reprinted by permission of Liverpool University Press.

The initiative that brought Lord Byron to sit for a portrait bust by the eminent Danish sculptor Bertel Thorvaldsen in May 1817 came from John Cam Hobhouse. The impetus to immortalise his friend in stone seems to have been purely personal. Whereas most of those close to Byron, whether as lovers or as friends, were happy to receive as a gift a miniature or even an engraving from a larger portrait, Hobhouse wanted something monumental, and tangible—and he was prepared to pay for it. He was, he liked to believe, Byron's dearest friend, and certainly he was the most selflessly devoted: 'a friend often tried and never found wanting', as Byron himself testified in that warmest of encomiums, the dedication to him of the fourth Canto of *Childe Harold's Pilgrimage*.[2] Hobhouse may also have been anticipating an eventuality in which he might never see Byron again. When they parted at Dover on 24 April 1816, on his leaving England as a self-imposed exile, Byron had hinted at a premonition that he might never return; Hobhouse noted the inference in his diary and the feeling of foreboding it evoked.[3] The choice of Thorvaldsen for the commission may have been influenced by the fee, which would probably have been less than the more celebrated Canova might have charged; but the latter, though still active, was approaching the end of his career and taking few commissions. Thorvaldsen, by contrast, was at the height of his powers; his studio, in which as many as forty men might be seen at work, was one of the sights of Rome to be visited by popes and princes; and his output was prodigious. His personality was no less formidable than his talent: tall and imposing in appearance and sardonic in manner, he was not a man to be overawed by his subjects, however famous and aristocratic. His encounter with Byron—the sittings were no less than that—inspired Thorvaldsen to produce one of his finest busts and the only great portrait of the poet.

Hobhouse's choice of the most austere of the Neo-Classical sculptors of the day must be seen in the context of his own enthusiasm for classical antiquity. By the time Byron arrived in Rome Hobhouse had spent nearly

---

2    *Byron: The Complete Poetical Works*, ed. by Jerome J. McGann, 7 vols (Oxford: Clarendon Press, 1980–93), II, 120–24. All subsequent references to Byron's poetry are to this edition, hereafter *CPW*.

3    Lord Broughton, *Recollections of a Long Life*, 6 vols (London: John Murray, 1909–11), I, 336, https://archive.org/details/recollectionsofa007946mbp

five months in the city, most of them in close study of the archaeological remains of Imperial Rome and of literary sources, both ancient and modern. His typically painstaking work is now remembered only for his contribution to the *Notes*, written jointly with Byron, accompanying the fourth Canto of *Childe Harold*; the book he was to publish in the following year containing material which could not be compressed into the *Notes* because of its 'disproportionate bulk' is now forgotten. Among the literary sources which he and Byron drew upon for the *Notes* was Johann Joachim Winckelmann, whose *Geschichhte der Kunst des Alterthums* published in 1764 imitated the essentially Romantic interpretation of the surviving artefacts of ancient Greece (or, more typically, Roman copies of lost originals) which came to be known as Neo-Classicism. Byron and Hobhouse read Winckelmann in an Italian translation, which they were to cite in the *Notes*. Another who almost certainly had read that translation was Thorvaldsen, who, as the brilliant gold-medallist of the Danish Academy, made the pilgrimage to Rome in 1797 where, almost inevitably, he fell under the influence of the prevailing Neo-Classical doctrines. In the words of his French biographer:

> The young Dane had hardly taken the first steps in the cause, which was destined to be so illustrious, when he met a fervent disciple of Winckelmann [...] Thorvaldsen was strongly encouraged by the learned archaeologist in his enthusiastic admiration for the grand style of antique statuary, and abandoned himself unreservedly to his inclination, thenceforward pursuing resolutely the course which was to lead to the complete development of his genius.[4]

The learned archaeologist was Georg Zöega, 'the Danish Winckelmann' and doyen of the artistic and literary circle of his fellow-countrymen in Rome. Whilst he recognised Thorvaldsen's outstanding talent as a sculptor, Zöega found him 'ignorant of everything outside art'. How is it possible, he complained, 'to study as he ought, if he does not know a word of Italian or French, if he has no acquaintance with history and mythology [...]?'[5] The young Bertel became a habitué of the Zöega household, where it seems he set about rapidly learning Italian. He formed a liaison with an Italian maidservant in the Zöegas' service, by

---

4    Eugène Plon, *Thorvaldsen: His Life and Works*, tr. by Mrs Cashel Hoey (London: Richard Bentley, 1874), p. 178.

5    Plon, *Thorvaldsen*, p. 22.

whom he was to have two children. And he adopted the Italian version of his name—Alberto—which he was to use professionally for the rest of his forty-year sojourn in the city.

Thorvaldsen's Danish biographer, J. M. Thiele, who knew the sculptor personally, believed that he found Byron's manner at their first meeting distasteful or even repulsive.[6] Thorvaldsen's own account, as told to an English visitor to his studio some ten years later, does not suggest antipathy so much as the wryly cynical amusement of a man approaching fifty at the antics of one not yet thirty. Byron 'appeared the first day in his atelier without any previous notice, wrapped up in his mantle, and with a look which was intended to impress upon the artist a powerful sentiment of his character. It was the first introduction; and Thorvaldsen from whom I heard the fact, admitted that the effect was commensurate with his wishes.'[7] But, if Thorvaldsen was not expecting Byron at that particular moment, he was not altogether surprised to see him for Hobhouse had prepared the way in a tactfully worded and even flattering letter. He wrote in the *lingua franca* of diplomatic and cosmopolitan society, which Thorvaldsen presumably had learned to read after twenty years in the company not just of scholars like Zöega but of his social superiors:

Milord Byron, *dont peut être vous auriez entendu parler comme du premier poète Anglais de nos jours est maintenant a Rôme. Je desire beaucoup qu'il puisse avoir un autre lien sure la postérité, pas moins durable que celui que lui ont fourni ses vers.—Voila pourquoi je le voudrais voir eternise par votre ciseau.*[8]

[[trans. by ed.] Lord Byron, whom you have perhaps heard spoken of as the leading English poet of our time, is now in Rome. I very much wish him to have a further hold on posterity, no less enduring than that which his verses have afforded him.—This is why I would like to see him immortalised by your chisel.]

Thorvaldsen's reply has been lost, so we do not know how many sittings there were or when they took place. The probability is that they were few, perhaps no more than two—an initial sketch in pencil and then the wet clay. He

---

6   M. R. Barnard, *The Life of Thorvaldsen, Collated from the Danish of J. M. Thiele* (London: Chapman and Hall, 1865), pp. 170, 171.

7   *New Monthly Magazine*, 19 (1827), 232.

8   J. M. Thiele, *Thorvaldsen in Rome, 1805–1819*, 4 vols (Copenhagen, 1852), I, 340.

worked in clay with extreme ardour, until he had set free from it the form which he had imagined, until he had given it the imprint of the thought which he had conceived. When it seemed to him that the clay had adequately rendered his ideas, he executed a plaster from it himself, which he generally finished very carefully: then he gave this to his workmen as a model, and it was their business to translate it in marble [...] he constantly superintended the work, frequently retouched it, sometimes finished it himself.[9]

Hobhouse was no less impressed by the sculptor's zest for the job; 'the artist worked *con amore*', he said, 'and told me it was the finest head he had ever under his hand.'[10] According to Thorvaldsen himself, recalling the events as an old man in conversation with his friend Hans Christian Andersen, he asserted his authority from the start:

'Oh, that was in Rome', said he, 'when I was about to make Byron's statue; he placed himself just opposite to me, and began immediately to assume quite another countenance to what was customary to him. "Will you not sit still?", said I; "but you must not make these faces". "It is my expression", said Byron. "Indeed?", said I, and then I made him as I wished, and everybody said, when it was finished, that I had hit the likeness. When Byron, however, saw it, he said, "It does not resemble me at all; I look more unhappy."' 'He was, above all things, so desirous of looking extremely unhappy', added Thorvaldsen, with a comic expression.[11]

Much has been made of Byron's remark, usually to the detriment of Thorvaldsen who, it is said, was of too humble a background and of too simple a nature to 'comprehend imaginary Misery'.[12] Mario Praz, the historian of Romantic modes, suggests a fundamental antipathy between the poet and the artist, not only personally, but as to their aesthetic assumptions. 'Byron', he declares, 'posed as a romantic, but Thorvaldsen carved in the Biedermeyer manner; he was alien to the portrayal of true sorrow: what then could he make of its imitation?'[13] There could hardly be a harsher dismissal of Thorvaldsen as an artist:

---

9   Plon, *Thorvaldsen*, p. 210.
10   Letter to John Murray, 7 December 1817 (John Murray Archive).
11   H. C. Andersen, *The True Story of My Life: A Sketch*, trans. by Mary Howitt (London: Longman, Brown, Green, and Longmans, 1847), p. 170.
12   Plon, *Thorvaldsen*, p. 53.
13   Mario Praz, *On Neo-Classicism* (London: Thames and Hudson, 1969), p. 273.

'biedermeyer' was no more than a term of abuse, the mid-nineteenth century equivalent of 'kitsch'. Those of us who know Byron from his letters to his close friends may suspect him of being facetiously ironical, not a little at his own expense. Thorvaldsen can be forgiven if he did not perceive such a nuance in his sitter's apparent rejection of his work.

Fig. 2.2 Bertel Thorvaldsen, *George Gordon Byron*, marble bust of Byron (1824). Thorvaldsens Museum, photograph by Jakob Faurvig, CC0, https://kataloget. thorvaldsensmuseum.dk/en/A256.

But the bust itself reveals that he had recognised in Byron a luminous and resolute spirit to be compared with that of a Greek god. As soon as he saw the plaster model, Byron must have been aware that he had undergone an apotheosis at the hands of the sculptor. He was slightly embarrassed, but at the same time he took a sheepish pride at being thus 'immortalised in marble while still alive'.[14] This sense of unease was revived some four years later, when he heard that a young American visitor had obtained a copy of the bust from Thorvaldsen.

---

14    Leslie A. Marchand, *Byron: A Biography*, 3 vols (London: John Murray, 1957), II, 693.

*I* would not pay the price of a Thorwaldsen [*sic*] bust for any human head & shoulders [...] If asked—*why* then I sate for my own—answer— that it was at the request particular of J. C. Hobhouse Esqre.—and for no one else.—A *picture* is a different matter—every body sits for their picture—but a bust looks like putting up pretensions to permanency— and smacks something of a hankering for *public* fame rather than private remembrance.[15]

Byron sometimes affected a kind of philistine indifference towards the fine arts, but his writings reveal that he could be as deeply and powerfully affected by painting and sculpture as by poetry. What he objected to was not art as such but the pretentiousness, as he regarded it, of the attitudes struck by those who professed to appreciate it. Writing from Florence, where he visited two galleries in the course of a visit of no more than a day *en route* to Rome, he had to admit that 'there are sculpture and painting—which for the first time gave me an idea of what people mean by their *cant* [...] about those two most artificial of the arts'.[16] He was overwhelmed by the visual experience of Rome, its architecture and, perhaps most of all, its sculpture: 'my first impressions are always strong and confused', he wrote soon after his arrival in the city, '& my Memory *selects* & reduces them to order—like distance in the landscape.'[17] In the fourth Canto of *Childe Harold*, which he started writing within a month of leaving 'the city of the soul', Byron painted Rome in brilliant *chiaroscuro*: men and gods, past and present seem to emerge suffused with light briefly to be seen before retreating into the shadows. Apollo, in the form of the Belvedere statue in the Vatican, inspired three stanzas which immediately precede the final immolation of *Childe Harold's Pilgrimage* now hardly distinguishable from the poet himself. 'The God of life, and poesy, and light— / [...] in his eye / And nostril beautiful disdain,' though 'made / By human hands [...]' still 'breathes the flame with which 'twas wrought'. Harold, by contrast, 'His wanderings done, his visions ebbing fast / [...] His

---

15 'Detached Thoughts', no. 25, Pisa, Oct.–Nov. 1821; *Byron's Letters and Journals*, ed. by Leslie A. Marchand, 13 vols (London: John Murray, 1973–94), IX, 21. All subsequent references to *Byron's Letters and Journals* are to this edition, hereafter *BLJ*.

16 Letter to John Murray, 26 April 1817; *BLJ* V, 218.

17 Letter to John Murray, 9 May 1817; *BLJ* V, 221.

shadow fades away into Destruction's mass'.[18] Byron's apostrophe to
Apollo carries echoes from Winckelmann.[19] In one of the most famous
passages in his *Geschichte* Winckelmann evokes the spirit of Apollo in
the most romantic terms. 'Apollo's lofty look, filled with consciousness
of power, seems to rise above his victory, and to gaze into infinity. Scorn
sits upon his lips, and his nostrils are swelling with suppressed anger,
which mounts even to the proud forehead [...].'[20] And Byron, like
Winckelmann, might well have said to himself in the presence of 'this
miracle of art, I feel myself transported to Delos and into the Lycaean
groves'.[21] Byron's debt to Winckelmann does not, of course, in any way
detract from the originality of his verse but his personal identification
with the Apollo, at least in some of its features, is clear. Scorn becomes
beautiful disdain—a facial expression of Byron's often commented on
by observers, and one which he may have tried to assume in front of
Thorvaldsen.

Whether or not Byron saw himself in the image of Apollo,
Thorvaldsen certainly did not regard himself as limited to any particular
classical model. He aspired towards a classical essence. In this search
for an archetype the sculptor would borrow certain features from the
antique portraits and combine details from a variety of types which were
originally very far removed from each other, in time and space, so as to
obtain a result serving his own purpose.[22] The Neo-Classical doctrine, in
Thorvaldsen's interpretation, could virtually submerge the individual
in the ideal. 'What you allow in portrait painting', he declared, 'is
inadmissible in sculpture, because a work of sculpture is a monument,
and just as the purpose of a monument cannot consist only in a record of
the actual event, thus a statue can achieve this and without reproducing
the features.'[23] Fortunately for posterity, the sculptor did not adhere to
this doctrine in its daunting austerity when faced with Byron. Indeed,

---

18  *Childe Harold*, IV, 161, 163, 164; CPW II, 178–79.
19  Hugh Honour, *Neoclassicism* (Harmondsworth: Penguin,1968), p. 61.
20  *Winckelmann: Writings on Art*, selected and ed. by David Irwin (London: Phaidon, 1972), p. 140.
21  Ibid.
22  Else K. Sass, 'The Classical Tradition in Later European Portraiture, with Special Regard to Thorvaldsen's Portraits', *Proceedings of the Second International Congress of Classical Studies*, vol. III: *The Classical Pattern of Modern Western Civilization, Portraiture* (Copenhagen: E. Munksgaard, 1957), p. 90.
23  Sass, 'Classical Tradition', p. 98.

his bust revealed the sitter's features in actuality, even in such a minor detail as his lobeless ears. In short it was a good likeness; Byron himself had to admit, if a little grudgingly, it was 'reckoned very good'.[24] When he sought to evoke the spirit of the poet—the ideal—Thorvaldsen did so without resort to extravagant mannerism; the eyes are only slightly uplifted, and their gaze suggests inner reflection rather than a search for inspiration from above. The lightly arched brows unite the separate features as might a frieze across the façade of a classical building. The head rests firmly and easily on a neck of great strength, though it is possible to perceive in the throat that alabaster beauty which was reputed to make women swoon. On first confronting the bust, at least in the original model, Byron's physical presence almost assaults the viewer. The sculptor recognised what all other portraitists had failed to see, so obsessed were they with the poetical ideal, that Byron was an athlete, a man capable of feats of physical skill and endurance. Only then perhaps does one become aware of a resonance that transcends the purely physical: the strength resides in the whole being, in the spirit made manifest in the flesh. And Byron's famous affirmation of the immortality of the spirit seems to transpire through the marble: 'But there is that within me which shall tire / Torture and Time, and breathe when I expire; [...]'[25]

Byron never saw his bust in marble; his favourable judgement was almost certainly based on a report from Hobhouse, who stayed on in Rome for nearly two months before joining his friend in Venice. During that time he called on Thorvaldsen in his studio and in the course of one of these visits he proposed a radical shift of emphasis away from the Greek ideal: he wanted to add a laurel wreath across the brow in the manner of a Roman military conqueror. The sculptor was not averse to this (he used such a motif on his bust of Napoleon), but the idea drew a furious response from Byron.

> I protest against & prohibit the '*laurels*'—which would be a most awkward assumption and anticipation of that which may never come to pass.—*You* would like them naturally because the verses won't do without them— but I won't have my head garnished like a Xmas pie with Holly—or a

---

24   Letter to John Murray, 4 June 1817; *BLJ* V, 235.
25   *Childe Harold*, IV, 137; *CPW* II, 170.

Cod's head and Fennel—or whatever the damned weed is they strew round it.—I wonder you should want me to be such a mountebank.[26]

So vehement a rejection of the trappings of military honours may seem surprising from one who no more than four V years ago had sat for his portrait wearing the dress of a warlike tribesman with a dagger in his belt. But Byron had changed since then and his underlying mood was sombre, barely concealed behind the flippant manner of the rest of his letter. He may, too, have been irritated by the verse which Hobhouse wanted to have inscribed at the base. In the face of such an onslaught Hobhouse could hardly persist; but he did not entirely relinquish the idea. '[W]hen the marble comes to England', he told John Murray later that year, 'I shall place a golden laurel round it in the ancient style, and if it is thought good enough suffix the following inscription, which may serve at last to tell the name of the portrait and allude to the existence of the artist, which very few lapidary inscriptions do.'[27] But the bust took an unconscionable time to reach England and Hobhouse's clumsy quatrain was never incised. One of Thorvaldsen's assistants simply chased the name *Byron* on the front of the herm. Thorvaldsen offered a choice of two modes: the herm, where the head and neck rest on a plain cubic base, or a bust proper where the upper shoulders and chest are revealed in a manner that is Roman rather than Greek. Hobhouse chose the former mode in which Winckelmann's neo-classical ideal of 'noble simplicity and serene greatness'[28] is perhaps more perfectly realised. But Hobhouse's frustrated desire to decorate the head of his hero reflects a general drift of taste from the formal and austere towards a naturalism which, at least in Britain, was ultimately to suffuse forms in a layer of glutinous sentiment.

'Chantrey does not think much of my bust of Lord Byron by Thorwaldsen [*sic*], nor does he think a great deal of Thorwaldsen'.[29] Hobhouse was on friendly personal terms with Francis Chantrey, the doyen of English sculptors, and he had a high regard for his opinions on sculpture in particular and art in general. His bust, his masterpiece, as

---

26    Letter to John Cam Hobhouse, 20 June 1817; *BLJ* V, 243.

27    Letter to John Murray, 7 December 1817 (John Murray Archive).

28    'Edle Binfalt und stille Grosse', quoted W. D. Robson-Scott, *The Younger Goethe and the Visual Arts* (Cambridge: Cambridge University Press, 1981), p. 18.

29    Broughton, *Recollections*, II, 176.

he justly believed it to be, had only recently arrived into his possession, nearly five years on from the heady days with Byron in Rome. Sensitive to a degree to anything which might imply, even indirectly, adverse criticism of his friend, Chantrey's remarks upset Hobhouse enough for him to record them in his diary. But he may, in his ruffled pride, have misunderstood Chantrey's words or read more into them than the sculptor had intended. For Chantrey had met Thorvaldsen at the latter's studio in Rome in October 1819 (he could have seen the Byron bust there) and, according to his Victorian biographer, who knew him far better than did Hobhouse, formed a high opinion of the Dane's work.[30] When, only a year or two later, Hobhouse was faced with the melancholy task of commissioning a statue as a monument to his dead hero it was to Chantrey that he turned.

The idea of a Byron monument to be erected in Poets' Corner of Westminster Abbey derived from Hobhouse's almost obsessive desire for official recognition and public acknowledgement of his friend's genius. He seemed to want a kind of canonisation as a symbol of secular acceptability. As an attitude to the authority of church and state it hardly accords with his Unitarian upbringing and political radicalism; but Hobhouse was in the process of sloughing off both, and in courting the establishment he invited rebuff. Undeterred by Dean Ireland's refusal to have Byron buried in the Abbey followed by a brusquely discourteous rejection of an effigy,[31] Hobhouse bided his time, waiting upon Ireland's death. He set up a Byron Monument Committee with John Murray as secretary, and solicited public subscription. They circularised members of both Houses of Parliament and appointed corresponding members abroad, but the result was disappointing. By 1829, when the fund was effectively closed, the sum in hand was more than three hundred pounds short of the £2,000 they needed.[32] It is not unlikely that Hobhouse consulted Chantrey in arriving at this figure, for he was his first choice for the commission. Again, Hobhouse was rebuffed: Chantrey refused the offer, probably because the fee

---

30  George Jones, R.A., *Sir Francis Chantrey, R.A.: Recollections of his Life, Practice, and Opinions* (London: E. Moxon, 1849), pp. 29, 30, https://archive.org/details/ sirfrancischantr00joneiala

31  Letter to John Cam Hobhouse, 17 Dec. 1834 (John Murray Archive).

32  Byron Monument, Account of Subscriptions Paid (John Murray Archive).

available was too low. And, as if to add insult to injury, he made a bust of Ireland in the same year. He had already done Wordsworth and was later to immortalise Southey in marble; he was to become a darling of the Court of William IV, and his work began to reflect a sycophantic appreciation of the great and the good.

Angered by Chantrey's shabby attitude, as he called it,[33] Hobhouse immediately wrote informally to Thorvaldsen, who responded with a warmth and generosity which put Chantrey to shame. The great sculptor, by then in his sixtieth year, regarded the commission as an honour:

> With an inexpressible pleasure I shall start work on a piece which will pass down to posterity the memory of the great genius already well enough known through his works and his talent. For my part, I assure you of my every care that this work shall be worthy of the Committee which orders it, and of the great poet whom I have known and whose loss I shall regret forever. In this task I shall have absolutely no regard for my personal interest, and thus I should like to make, if you wish, for this price (£1,000 sterling) a bas relief on the pedestal. [...] As soon as I have your reply, I shall start work on a monument, in order to finish it as soon as possible.[34]

It is clear that Thorvaldsen's admiration for Byron was deep seated and more than just a response to the hero of Greek independence, which his biographers have tended to emphasise. A native of a country which fought as an ally of Napoleon; an artist whose firm adherence to the Neo-Classical ideal identified him with the art of Revolutionary France, Thorvaldsen perhaps recognised in Byron the spirit his country's rulers feared and wanted to suppress. He would affirm that spirit in a monument which, like the poet's own works, would live when his detractors were long forgotten.

The monument committee formally accepted Thorvaldsen's offer in November 1829 and, true to his word, the sculptor set to work quickly; his first rough sketches on paper were made in August of the following year and work began on the marble in 1831.

---

33   John Cam Hobhouse, letter to John Murray, 31 Aug. 1829 (John Murray Archive).
34   Letter from Bertel Thorvaldsen to John Cam Hobhouse, 25 July 1829 (from a transcription of the original in the John Murray Archive).

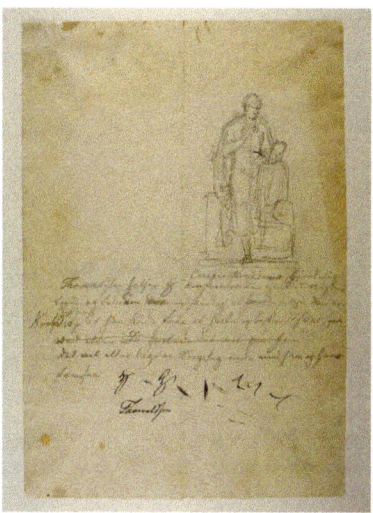

Fig. 2.3 Bertel Thorvaldsen, *Monument for George Gordon Byron*, pencil sketch of Byron statue (1830). Thorvaldsens Museum, photograph by Helle Nanny Brendstrup, CC0, https://kataloget.thorvaldsensmuseum.dk/en/C352.

Fig. 2.4 Bertel Thorvaldsen, *Monument for George Gordon Byron with the Relief the Genius of Poetry on the Plinth*, pencil sketch of Byron statue and relief for the plinth (1830–31). Thorvaldsens Museum, photograph by Jakob Faurvig, CC0, https://kataloget.thorvaldsensmuseum.dk/en/C350r.

He must have considered many options for the memorial, the most
obvious of which, perhaps, was the heroic. That was the image chosen
by the Belgian painter Joseph Odevaere (a former pupil of J.-L. David in
Paris) in his painting of 1826; the hero as a classical nude stretched out
on his death bed. Thorvaldsen's approach was to show 'the ideal picture
of a gifted poet, as antiquity would present the very muse of poetry'.[35]
The final outcome, achieved only after some searching, was a figure of
great originality, imbued with vitality though quietly reflective, and yet
clearly a man of his own time—and indeed of our time.

The statue is replete with references to classical antiquity. Byron is
depicted in a seated position which is said to have been partly derived
from two statues of Greek philosophers in the Vatican, copies of which
Thorvaldsen kept in his studio.[36] The figure rests amongst the debris
of an Attic temple with a fragment of a frieze as a seat and a broken
column, fluted in the Doric style, supporting the feet. On either side of
the frieze, Thorvaldsen carved in relief the owl of Minerva and the lyre
of Apollo, possibly taken from the images on his extensive collection of
Attic coins. After such a clutter of symbols on the statue proper, the base
seems refreshingly plain; only the forward-facing side is decorated, and
there the sculptor carved an exquisite bas-relief representing the Genius
of poetry and song, Apollo himself.

A lesser sculptor than Thorvaldsen might have allowed the weight
of antique allusion to overwhelm the figure itself; and indeed his first
essay, as revealed in a bozzetto of 1830, is singularly inert. In this small
gesso model Byron is seated, holding a book in his left hand which rests
on his knee, which in turn is propped up by a foot on the broken column.
Each of these features was eventually to appear in the finished work; but
in the model the head faces directly to the front, as in the original bust.
Thorvaldsen's decision, which must have been made in the same year, to
turn the head half right across the shoulders introduced the suggestion
of tension, which is the source of the astonishing vitality that suffuses
the effigy from top to toe. Other features contribute to the effect, most
importantly the graceful but powerful drapery which the sculptor was
able to introduce by wrapping the figure in a riding cloak. Thorvaldsen
had seen Byron so dressed as he first entered his studio thirteen years

---

35   Wilhelm Wanscher, *Artes*, tome 1 (Copenhagen, 1932), p. 308.
36   Sass, 'Classical Tradition', p. 76.

earlier; the figure he now created was that of the poet as a man still young and in his full vigour.

This, then, is the Byron of the grand tour, seated among the 'shatter'd splendour' of ancient Greece and, perhaps, anticipating the day when the past glory might 'vanquish Time and Fate' and renew itself in our time.[37]

Fig. 2.5 Bertel Thorvaldsen, *Monument to George Gordon Byron*, full-size plaster model of statue of Byron (May 1831). Thorvaldsens Museum, photograph by Jakob Faurvig, CC0, https://kataloget.thorvaldsensmuseum.dk/en/A130.

As if to emphasise the poet, rather than the hero, Thorvaldsen has him holding a copy of *Childe Harold* whilst he ponders the verse—pen in hand. And, if evidence were needed, the statue itself reveals the sculptor's acquaintanceship with at least the earlier Cantos of Byron's great poem,—even if he read it, as he could only have done, in translation. But, although there is a lightness of spirit about the effigy he created, Thorvaldsen has not romanticised Byron. The power and strength of the

---

37    Words supposedly uttered by Newton shortly before his death in 1727, reported
       by Joseph Spence in *Anecdotes, Observations and Characters, of Books and Men* (1820),
       I, 158; referred to in *Don Juan*, Canto VII, 5; *CPW* V, 338.

bust now spread through the whole figure: the capability of soldierly action is latent.

The fatal consequence of such action is, however, only hinted at in a visual metaphor, explicit enough in itself, which is half hidden behind the broken column. There, to the left of the figure, which faces away from it, Thorvaldsen placed a human skull; and, as if to emphasise the reference to Byron, he allowed folds of his cloak to come to rest upon it.

Fig. 2.6 Bertel Thorvaldsen, statue of Byron in the Wren Library, showing the owl of Minerva and the skull as memento mori. Photograph courtesy of Trinity College, Cambridge.

Whilst the sculptor's intention is clear, the introduction of yet another symbol, of a very different kind from the others, only serves to confuse; the effect is the antithesis of noble simplicity. The skull as a reminder of the mortality of the flesh is far from classical in spirit; no Attic sculptor, for whom men and gods inhabited one cosmos, could have countenanced it. Thorvaldsen's eclecticism in this respect does not diminish the power of this masterpiece of his later years. Like other artists trained in the Neo-Classical aesthetic, most notably Delacroix, the imperatives of the times—and in this case a tempestuous genius as a subject—demanded of Thorvaldsen that he should wrestle with the conventional forms handed down to him; and much of the strength of the statue stems from his struggle. Byron himself would surely have understood. He too, however much he might revere the Augustan poetical mode, found that his genius could not be so trammelled.

The statue arrived by cargo vessel from Rome in November 1834 and Hobhouse went down to the docks to deal with formalities at HM Customs and Excise, in one of whose warehouses it was stored. It was to stay there for ten years. The sole reason for this ridiculous state of affairs was Hobhouse and his committee's insistence that the statue should go to the Abbey and the stubborn refusal of an Evangelical-minded clergy to have the poet within its precincts. There was no point in looking to a haven in St Paul's, if only because the Bishop of London, the Rt Revd Charles Blomfield, regarded Byron as a species of Infidel and was to use the privileged platform of the House of Lords to execrate his name when the matter was briefly debated there in June 1844.[38] His experience as an undergraduate contemporary of Byron at Trinity College, Cambridge may perhaps have affected his judgement.

In his second letter to Thorvaldsen, Hobhouse had mentioned two other possible destinations for the Byron monument, namely the British Museum and the National Gallery. There is however no evidence of any approach being made to the authorities of either of these institutions, where the religious impediment could hardly have been raised. It is difficult to believe that they were seriously considered, at least by Hobhouse. There is, too, no evidence that Thorvaldsen was consulted or even informed about the course of events, though he could hardly have been indifferent to the fate of the work which had engaged his generous sympathy no less than his skill. His monument to Byron still lay in a crate in a London warehouse, when Thorvaldsen himself laden with honours, died in his native city in the spring of 1844.

The initiative that was to resolve the problem and, incidentally, to rescue Hobhouse and his committee from their embarrassing position came from Trinity College. As early as March 1840, a graduate member of the college wrote to the Senior Tutor with a proposal that the statue should be placed in the college itself or in the University's new museum, The Fitzwilliam, then still under construction. Nothing came of this approach and the matter hung fire for another three years. Undeterred, this persistent young man, whose name, Charles De La

---

38   *The Times*, 15 June 1844.

Pryme, deserves to be remembered, wrote to the Master himself, Dr
Whewell, who responded very warmly. He clearly wanted the statue for
the college; a formal application was made on behalf of the Fellows to
the subscription committee in April 1843.[39] De La Pryme was too young
to have known Byron, but his father must have remembered him for he
was a Fellow of the College when the poet was an undergraduate. In
1832 he was elected a Member of Parliament for the city of Cambridge
in the Whig interest, and in that capacity he was to work closely with
Hobhouse in the House of Commons. It is highly likely therefore that
Hobhouse knew of the approach to Trinity College from the beginning;
he was to use it as an option which he could hold in reserve while he
played politics with the Abbey. He was to persist almost to the point of
public humiliation; not until July 1844 did he agree to the acceptance of
the offer from Trinity. Even then he had to assert the righteousness of
his cause in a privately printed and anonymous pamphlet in which he
argued his case at tedious length.[40]

The pamphlet is memorable only for Hobhouse's appreciation of
Byron, a kind of belated obituary, almost as moving for its expression
of heartfelt love for his friend as for his evocation of the man himself.
It does much to explain his prolonged and tenacious struggle with the
Abbey: if only the truth were known as he knew it, even the prejudices
of a hostile clergy would be dispelled and the statue welcomed within
their precincts. He never really came to terms with his defeat. For him
Trinity was a place of exile of Byron in effigy comparable, as a symbol
of rejection, with the real exile thirty years earlier; and in a sense he
was right. When the statue finally reached the college and was hoisted
in the Wren Library on October 18th, 1845, there was no ceremony to
mark the event. Byron's reputation was sinking into a slough of moral
disapproval and incomprehension of his genius from which it was not to
be rescued for over a century, and Thorvaldsen's monument was largely
unappreciated, if not forgotten.

---

39   The correspondence was summarised by the then Librarian, Dr Robert Sinker, in
     *Notes and Queries*, 6.4 (December 1881), 421–23, https://babel.hathitrust.org/cgi/
     pt?id=mdp.39015020441013&seq=612.
40   Anon. [John Cam Hobhouse], *Remarks on the Exclusion of Lord Byron's Monument
     from Westminster Abbey*, n.d. [London, 1844].

Fig. 2.7 Photograph of the Byron statue shortly after its installation in the Wren Library in 1845. Courtesy of Trinity College, Cambridge (Add.PG.13[5]).

Only now perhaps can we recognise the utter appropriateness of its setting. Sir Christopher Wren's library at Trinity is one of the architect's masterpieces, his finest secular building. To view the statue there in the constantly changing light from the vast windows is to experience something of the spirit of Enlightenment and Reason which, however fiercely assailed, always remained Byron's 'last and only place / Of refuge'.[41]

---

41    *Childe Harold*, IV, 127; *CPW* II, 166.

# 3. On the Statue of Lord Byron by Thorwaldsen[1] in Trinity College Library, Cambridge

## Charles Tennyson Turner (1808–1879)

'Tis strange that I, who haply might have met
Thy living self—who sought to hide the flaws
In thy great fame, and, though I ne'er had set
Eyes on thee, heard thee singing without pause,
And longed to see thee, should, alas! detect
The Thyrza-sorrow first on sculptured brows,
And know thee best in marble! Fate allows
But this poor intercourse; high and erect
Thou hold'st thy head, whose forward glance beholds
All forms that throng this learned vestibule;
Women and men, and boys and girls from school,
Who gaze with admiration all unchecked
On thy proud lips, and garment's moveless folds,
So still, so calm, so purely beautiful!

This sonnet was reprinted, along with three others, in the anthology *Trinity Poets*, ed. by Angela Leighton and Adrian Poole (Manchester: Carcanet, 2017), p. 164, with a note on the author, an abbreviated version of which here follows:

Charles Turner (formerly Tennyson), elder brother of Alfred, was admitted to Trinity in 1827. His first independent volume, *Sonnets and Fugitive Pieces* (1830), was much admired by Coleridge. After graduating in 1832, he was ordained deacon, and then priest in 1833. When a

---

1    Bertel Thorvaldsen or Thorwaldsen (*c.*1770–1844), Danish sculptor.

©2024 Adrian Poole, CC BY-NC 4.0    https://doi.org/10.11647/OBP.0399.03

great-uncle died in 1835, Charles inherited much of his property, changing his name from Tennyson to Turner, though widely referred to as 'Charles Tennyson Turner'. A year later he married Louisa Sellwood, whose sister Emily would marry his brother, Alfred. The marriage between Charles and Louisa was severely tested by his opium addiction; they separated and were reunited in 1849. He seems to have overcome his addiction, and started to write poetry again. In 1864 he published *Sonnets*, followed by *Small Tableaux* (1868) and *Sonnets, Lyrics, and Translations* (1873). In 1866 ill-health forced him to retire from active ministry, and he died thirteen years later. Though his was an often unhappy life, Charles seems to have found in the small compass of the sonnet a form in which to escape the shadow of his much more famous brother.

# 4. Poets and Travellers[1]

## William St Clair

Lord Byron was twenty-one and not yet famous when he wrote *English Bards and Scotch Reviewers* shortly before he set out on his voyage to the Mediterranean.[2] Since there was scarcely a single contemporary writer, famous or obscure, who escaped his satirical scorn, the manuscript was turned down by ten or more regular London publishers.[3] Eventually Byron contracted with James Cawthorn, a fringe publisher, for an edition of 1,000 copies to be published anonymously. Byron later authorized a second edition with amendments, then a third and a fourth, each of 1,000 copies, all of which acknowledged his authorship.

Soon after his return from his travels, when he realized that *English Bards and Scotch Reviewers* had been unfair to many authors who were now his friends, he refused Cawthorn permission to print a fifth edition, and ordered the poem to be suppressed. This made little difference. The price of second-hand copies soared. An advertisement of 1818 by a Paris pirate publisher claimed that 'this work is so scarce in London that copies

---

1    Published in *Lord Elgin and the Marbles: The Controversial History of the Parthenon Sculptures*, 3rd revised edn (Oxford and New York: Oxford University Press, 1998), Chapter 17, pp. 80–200. Reprinted by permission of David St Clair.

2    The main features of the early publication history are noted by Thomas James Wise, *A Bibliography of the Writings in Verse and Prose of George Gordon, Lord Byron* (London: private circulation, 1933). Repr. edn (Folkestone, Kent: Dawsons of Pall Mall), https://archive.org/details/bibliographyofwr0002wise_t1q8/page/n5/mode/2up.

3    '[T]en or *twelve*' according to Byron's letter of 25 December 1822, *Byron's Letters and Journals*, ed. by Leslie A. Marchand, 13 vols (London: John Murray, 1973–94), X, 70. All subsequent references to *Byron's Letters and Journals* are to this edition, hereafter *BLJ*. The reason for Longman's refusal is confirmed in a letter to Revd Mr Card, 8 May 1815, 'some of our friends were hard treated in it' (Longman archives, University of Reading Library, 99/98).

    https://doi.org/10.11647/OBP.0399.04

have been sold for five guineas and upwards'.[4] Shelley's friend Thomas
Jefferson Hogg noted that the book 'became so exceedingly scarce that
a large price was often given for a copy, and some curious people even
took the trouble to transcribe it'.[5] Many manuscript copies written by
professional copyists appeared on the market.[6] When an Irish publisher
put on sale a printed pirated edition Cawthorn took legal proceedings
to have him stopped. But the real pirate was Cawthorn himself. Denied
permission to print a fifth edition, he went on reprinting third and fourth
editions. About twenty such fakes have been identified, all claiming on
the title-page to have been issued in 1810 or 1811, but all reprints and all
manufactured from paper on which the manufacturing dates of 1812,
1815, 1816, 1817, 1818, and 1819 are clearly visible in the watermarks.[7]

Over the first ten years after publication Cawthorn probably sold
about 20,000 copies of *English Bards*. By the standards of the day, the
poem was a runaway best-seller. Many of the readers, we can be sure,
were the members of London fashionable society who patronized
the large circulating library in London which was Cawthorn's main
business. Indeed there can have been few men or women among the
upper and middle classes who did not read it. By the 1820s, because
the ownership of the copyright was uncertain, *English Bards and Scotch
Reviewers* was reprinted by other publishers and became available to an
even wider readership in innumerable cheaper editions.

Towards the end of the poem, as an aside from the scorn at the
writers, Byron took a swipe at the antiquarians:

> Let ABERDEEN and ELGIN still pursue
> The shade of fame through regions of Virtu;
> Waste useless thousands on their Phidian freaks,

---

4   Advertisements by A. and W. Galignani in copies of books published by the firm.
    Five guineas would imply a premium of over 2,000 per cent above Cawthorn's
    price of five shillings, itself not cheap.

5   Thomas Jefferson Hogg, *The Life of Percy Bysshe Shelley*, 2 vols (London:
    Edward Moxon, 1858), I, 300, https://www.google.co.uk/books/edition/
    The_Life_of_Percy_Bysshe_Shelley/O18JAAAAQAAJ?hl=en&gbpv=1

6   They are still commonly found. Most were written in expensive morocco
    notebooks, and carefully reproduce the title-page, the preface, and the notes as
    well as the verse.

7   There are also fakes of the first edition, and of the third edition with paper
    watermarked 1808, copies in the author's collection (now in Trinity College
    Library).

Mis-shapen monuments, and maimed antiques;
And make their grand saloons a general mart
For all the mutilated blocks of art:[8]

In a footnote he added 'Lord Elgin would fain persuade us that all the figures, with and without noses, in his stoneshop are the work of Phidias! "Credat Judaeus!"'

Few readers of the poem outside art circles are likely to have realized that Byron was endorsing the Payne Knight view that the claims made for the Parthenon sculptures were exaggerated.[9] Byron's sneer at Lord Elgin's syphilitic nose, on the other hand, probably caused titters and sniggers among those in the know. Another rhyme about Lord Elgin's noseless marbles is known to have been widely repeated, and perhaps invented, by Byron.

Noseless himself, he brings home noseless blocks,
To show at once the ravages of time and pox.[10]

On his way back from Greece in 1811, Byron acted as courier for a letter from Lusieri to Elgin. On 29 July 1811, Elgin paid a personal call on him at his hotel in order to thank him, and when he found him not at home, wrote a letter asking for a meeting:

I did myself the honor of calling upon your Lordship this morning, to thank you for the letter you was so good as [to] bring for me from Malta—and with a desire of enquiring into the nature of Lusieri's late acquisitions & operations at Athens, in regard to which I have not

---

8    *English Bards and Scotch Reviewers*, lines 1027–32, in Byron: *The Complete Poetical Works*, ed. by Jerome J. McGann, 7 vols (Oxford: Clarendon Press, 1980–93), I, 261. All subsequent references to Byron's poetry are to this edition, hereafter *CPW*.

9    [ed.: In a previous chapter, St Clair described Richard Payne Knight (1750–1824) as 'chief spokesman for the art collectors, the art patrons, and the art connoisseurs'. Payne Knight told Lord Elgin that his marbles were over-rated—not Greek but Roman of the time of Hadrian, and spent 'ten years proclaiming that the sculptures of the Parthenon were inferior works, mere architectural decoration' (*Lord Elgin*, pp. 167–69).]

10   *CPW* VII, 103. The couplet was attributed to Martin Archer Shee but is not included in his *Rhymes on Art* (London: H. Ebers, 1805). For Byron quoting it, see also *Medwin's Conversations of Lord Byron*, ed. by Ernest J. Lovell Jr. (Princeton, NJ: Princeton University Press, 1966), p. 211. The attribution to Byron is made in some unreliable editions of his works. A short poem in Latin, *CPW* I, 330, repeats the satire of the revenge of Venus which is among the main themes of *The Curse of Minerva*, discussed below.

received any recent information. If your Lordship would do me the favor of naming any time, when I could, without inconvenience to you, wait upon you for that purpose, I should be greatly indebted to you.[11]

Byron responded to this request from his fellow peer in a letter, now lost, in which he gave a report about Lusieri's activities. Something of the contents and friendly respectful tone of the letter can be deduced from a second letter which Lord Elgin wrote in reply on 31 July:

> I am under a very great obligation indeed to your Lordship for the trouble you have taken on my application to you. And I have extreme reluctance in being further importunate, but in truth, the circumstance of your not being a collector makes me attach double value to the opinion you may have formed on the objects of the researches still carrying on for me at Athens, and I confess I should esteem it a very essential favor to be allowed a few minutes conversation with your Lordship in those matters.—If you would therefore permit me, & I hear nothing to the Contrary from you—I would beg leave to do myself the honor of waiting upon you about Eleven o'c tomorrow forenoon; otherwise at any other time you might prefer.[12]

It was on that day or the next that Byron received news that his mother was seriously ill and he left London immediately. He probably never met Elgin, nor had he any wish to do so. As he wrote to his friend Hobhouse on 31 July when he was still in London and after he had received Elgin's second letter:

> Lord Elgin has been teazing to see me these last four days, I wrote to him at his request all I knew about his robberies, & at last have written to say that as it is my intention to publish (in Childe Harold) on that topic, I thought proper since he insisted on seeing me to give him notice, that he might not have an opportunity of accusing me of double dealing afterwards.[13]

Whatever the warning was there was little that Elgin could do, nor could he ever have guessed that the young lord who had used his painter as his guide to Athens and had sailed in his ship from Greece

---

11   John Murray archives. Not previously published or known. Original spelling retained.

12   Ibid. Not previously published or known.

13   Letter to Hobhouse, 31 July 1811, in *BLJ* II, 65–66.

to Malta was destined to do him more damage than Payne Knight or Napoleon Bonaparte.

*Childe Harold's Pilgrimage, a Romaunt*, the long poem which Byron had been composing during his travels, was turned down by Longman and by Constable, the two leading literary publishers of the time, because it contained attacks on Lord Elgin. William Miller, who published Elgin's *Memorandum*, also turned it down, and there may have been others.[14] It was only with the help of a friend with connections in the literary world that, after some months of disappointment, Byron managed to place it with John Murray, who was then still an outside publisher with little to lose.[15] The result was one of the most astonishing events in English literary history.

Within three days of the book's publication on about 1 March 1812 the first edition of 500 copies was sold out. Over the next two years 13,000 copies were printed and sold, mostly to members of the British aristocracy and gentry, to circulating libraries, to book clubs, and increasingly abroad.[16] With *Childe Harold*, as he used to say, Byron woke up and found himself famous. The hostesses of London crowded him with invitations, fashionable young ladies vied for his attentions, the Prince Regent joined in the congratulations, and the literary world at once forgave the youthful excesses of *English Bards*. The scurrilous versifier had become a great romantic poet, and *Childe Harold's Pilgrimage* was eagerly read in every drawing-room in England. It was to become one of the most admired and most read poems of the nineteenth century.[17]

---

14    Thomas Moore's *Letters and Journals of Lord Byron* (London: Murray, 1830), Chapter 11.

15    That Constable was among the publishers who rejected *Childe Harold's Pilgrimage* is shown by Byron's reference to 'the Crafty' in his letter of 25 December 1882, *BLJ* X, 70, not previously identified as a reference to Constable as far as I know. For Constable as 'the Crafty' see Mrs Oliphant, *Annals of a Publishing House: William Blackwood and his sons, their magazine and friends*, 2 vols (Edinburgh and London: Blackwood, 1897–98), I, 121, and J. G. Lockhart, *The Life of Sir Walter Scott, Bart*, one-volume edition (London: Adam & Charles Black, 1893), p. 167.

16    Murray archives. In order to give the book-buying public the impression that the book was selling even more rapidly than was the case Murray, by changing the title pages, pretended that there were ten editions before the end of 1814, although there were only six.

17    William St Clair, 'The Impact of Byron's Writings: An Evaluative Approach', in *Byron, Augustan and Romantic*, ed. by Andrew Rutherford (Basingstoke: Macmillan, 1990), pp. 1–25.

Only once in the body of the poem did *Childe Harold's Pilgrimage* attack a living individual. At the beginning of Canto II Childe Harold has arrived in Greece. Sitting upon a 'massy stone, the marble column's yet unshaken base' and contemplating the ruins of the Parthenon, his melancholy gives way to anger.

> But who, of all the plunderers of yon fane
> On high, where Pallas linger'd, loth to flee
> The latest relic of her ancient reign;
> The last, the worst, dull spoiler, who was he?
> Blush, Caledonia! such thy son could be!
> England! I joy no child he was of thine:
> Thy free-born men should spare what once was free;
> Yet they could violate each saddening shrine,
> And bear these altars o'er the long-reluctant brine.

> But most the modern Pict's ignoble boast,
> To rive what Goth, and Turk, and Time hath spar'd:
> Cold as the crags upon his native coast,
> His mind as barren and his heart as hard,
> Is he whose head conceiv'd, whose hand prepar'd,
> Aught to displace Athena's poor remains:
> Her sons too weak the sacred shrine to guard,
> Yet felt some portion of their mother's pains,
> And never knew, till then, the weight of Despot's chains.

> What! shall it e'er be said by British tongue,
> Albion was happy in Athena's tears?
> Though in thy name the slaves her bosom wrung,
> Tell not the deed to blushing Europe's ears;
> The ocean queen, the free Britannia bears
> The last poor plunder from a bleeding land:
> Yes, she, whose gen'rous aid her name endears,
> Tore down those remnants with a Harpy's hand,
> Which envious Eld forbore, and tyrants left to stand.

> Where was thine Aegis, Pallas! that appall'd
> Stern Alaric and Havoc on their way?
> Where Peleus' son? whom Hell in vain enthrall'd,
> His shade from Hades upon that dread day,
> Bursting to light in terrible array!
> What? could not Pluto spare the chief once more,
> To scare a second robber from his prey?
> Idly he wander'd on the Stygian shore,
> Nor now preserv'd the walls he lov'd to shield before.

Cold is the heart, fair Greece! that looks on thee,
Nor feels as lovers o'er the dust they lov'd;
Dull is the eye that will not weep to see
Thy walls defac'd, thy mouldering shrines remov'd
By British hands, which it had best behov'd
To guard those relics ne'er to be restor'd.
Curst be the hour when from their isle they rov'd,
And once again thy hapless bosom gor'd,
And snatch'd thy shrinking Gods to northern climes abhorr'd![18]

With the publication of these verses, the controversy over the Elgin Marbles moved to a new battlefield. No longer did the conversation turn on the dry academic question of whether the marbles were truly 'Phidian' or not. Now the question was what right had Elgin to remove the precious heritage of a proud nation, what right had he to raise his hand against a building that had stood for over two thousand years. The Elgin Marbles had now become a symbol, of Greece's ignominious slavery, of Europe's failure to help her, and of Britain's overweening pride. The land of Greece, with its intensely beautiful landscape and clear atmosphere, offered a powerful romantic fantasy—classical ruins with goats in the foreground, turbaned pashas, inscrutable and cruel, smoking their long pipes, black-eyed girls, young, passionate, and open. The mixture of ancient classicism and oriental exoticism made a strong appeal to the peoples of Northern Europe and North America who could visit the Mediterranean only in their imaginations.

After *Childe Harold* Byron published a rapid succession of other poems with Greek themes, *The Giaour*, *The Bride of Abydos*, *The Corsair*, *The Siege of Corinth*, all of which were immensely popular both at home and abroad, then and later. By the time the battle of Waterloo brought the long wars to an end in 1815 Byron was a European figure, almost as famous as Napoleon.

Much of the poem is about the present condition of the countries through which the poet made his pilgrimage. The Greeks are slaves, Byron proclaimed. And it is no good the Greeks looking to foreigners to help them, what Greece needs is a violent revolution. The Greeks will never be free until they imitate their ancient ancestors.

---

18   *Childe Harold*, Canto II, 11–15; *CPW* II, 47–49.

> When riseth Lacedemon's hardihood,
> When Thebes Epaminondas rears again,
> When Athens' children are with hearts endued,
> When Grecian mother shall give birth to men,
> Then may'st thou be restored; but not till then.[19]

There is contempt for the Modern Greeks for their ignorance and lack of patriotism:

> Shrine of the mighty! can it be,
> That this is all remains of thee?
> Approach thou craven crouching slave—
> Say, is this not Thermopylae?
> These waters blue that round you lave
> O servile offspring of the free—
> Pronounce what sea, what shore is this?
> The gulf, the rock of Salamis![20]

No need to remind a European readership of the associations of these names. The Modern Greeks, it is implicitly assumed, are the descendants of the Ancient Greeks, degenerate slaves, passively accepting their humiliation among the monuments of their former greatness. The word 'lave' exists in romantic poetry mainly to provide a rhyme for 'slave'.

Byron was an example of a type which was already a familiar feature of the Greek scene, the milordos or travelling gentleman. Greeks and Turks could understand how it might be necessary, from time to time, to go to the trouble, expense, and considerable danger of travel for the sake of business or to make a pilgrimage. But to travel for pleasure, or to look at ruins, that was a western European madness. The travellers, whether British, French, or from other countries necessarily saw the country through eyes that had been pre-set by their education in the classics. Clutching their copies of Plutarch and Pausanias, they mostly knew nothing of the history of the country after the death of Alexander the Great. They simply assumed that the Modern Greeks were the linear descendants of the ancients, although much debased by foreign occupation, without bothering too much about the facts or the implications. They looked carefully at Greek faces to see if they

---

19    *Childe Harold*, Canto II, 84; CPW II, 72.
20    *The Giaour*, lines 106–13; CPW III, 43.

could find the Grecian profiles shown in ancient vases. They wondered whether Modern Greek customs such as the siesta and love of arguing, were survivals from ancient times.

Byron's ideas about Greece were not new. They had been constructed by a succession of travellers and writers mainly British and French, during the eighteenth century.[21] The notion that Greeks might overthrow their Turkish rulers and take their place among the nations of modern Europe was also already a commonplace among the literatures of Europe, and had been adopted by some prominent Greek writers living abroad. But not until Byron had the ideology of philhellenism been expressed with such power or carried so widely all over the Western word. Byron shared in the glamour of Greece, but Greece in its turn was carried along by the glamour of Byron, with innumerable painting and engravings giving a visual reinforcement to the philhellenic myth.[22]

Under the conventions of the long romantic poem, as it was developed in Scotland and England by Sir Walter Scott, Lord Byron, Thomas Moore, and others, it was the custom to complement the verse part of the poem with explanatory and historical prose notes which were not only of direct interest to readers in their own right but added authority and legitimacy to the verse. With the verse appealing to the emotions and the prose to the intellect, a long romantic poem could thus not only address the whole mind of the reader, but it could also offer cumulative, and occasionally alternative, ways of reading and of understanding the main text. In the case of *Childe Harold's Pilgrimage, a Romaunt*, more than half of the book was taken up with writings other than the verse narrative. Although contemporary readers of *Childe Harold's Pilgrimage* could thus, if they wished, read the work as an impassioned polemic,

---

21  See Terence Spencer, *Fair Greece, Sad Relic: Literary Philhellenism from Shakespeare to Byron* (London: Weidenfeld & Nicholson, 1954), and the early chapters and appendix of William St Clair, *That Greece Might Still Be Free: The Philhellenes in the War of Independence*, new edition (Cambridge: Open Book Publishers, 2008, https://www.openbookpublishers.com/books/10.11647/obp.0001), which describe, and to some extent quantify, the books and reading by which the philhellenic myth was consolidated and diffused.

22  See especially Fani-Maria Tsigakou, *The Rediscovery of Greece: Travellers and Romantics in the Nineteenth Century* (London: Fine Art Society, 1979) and *Through Romantic Eyes: European images of nineteenth-century Greece from the Benaki Museum, Athens* (Athens, 1991), and the many gorgeous illustrations in *The Parthenon and its Impact in Modern Times*, ed. by Panayotis Tournikiotis (Athens: Melissa, c. 1994).

it appeared at the same time as a carefully considered and researched factual account by a highly educated traveller who had been on the spot and who knew both ancient and modern Greek.[23]

Many of the notes in *Childe Harold's Pilgrimage* related to Lord Elgin.

> We can all feel, or imagine, the regret with which the ruins of cities, once the capitals of empires, are beheld; the reflections suggested by such objects are too trite to require recapitulation. But never did the littleness of man, and the vanity of his very best virtues, of patriotism to exalt, and of valour to defend his country, appear more conspicuous than in the record of what Athens was, and the certainty of what she now is. This theatre of contention between mighty factions, of the struggles of orators, the exaltation and deposition of tyrants, the triumph and punishment of generals, is now become a scene of petty intrigue and perpetual disturbance, between the bickering agents of certain British nobility and gentry. 'The wild foxes, the owls and serpents in the ruins of Babylon', were surely less degrading than such inhabitants. The Turks have the plea of conquest for their tyranny, and the Greeks have only suffered the fortune of war, incidental to the bravest; but how are the mighty fallen, when two painters contest the privilege of plundering the Parthenon, and triumph in turn, according to the tenor of each succeeding firman![24] Sylla could but punish, Philip subdue, and Xerxes burn Athens, but it remained for the paltry Antiquarian, and his despicable agents, to render her contemptible as himself and his pursuits.[25]

In another passage, written on 3 January 1810, before Lusieri's ship had sailed he declared:

---

23    Without going back to the early editions, especially those published before 1816 when *Childe Harold's Pilgrimage, Canto the Third*, was published as a separate book, it is hard for present-day readers to recapture a reliable sense of how *Childe Harold's Pilgrimage: A Romaunt*, was read, appreciated, and understood in the years immediately after it was published. With the development, in Victorian times, of the romantic notion that it was only the verse part of the book which constituted the 'poem', most editions, including the *Complete Poetical Works*, have tended to cut back the long passages of accompanying prose or to treat them, anachronistically, as if they were equivalent to scholarly editorial annotations to a prime text. Many modern editions omit them altogether. At the time when the work was first read, *Childe Harold's Pilgrimage, A Romaunt*, with its voluminous factual supporting and illustrative information about the antiquities, the state of literature, the history, and the political options open to the Greeks, probably reinforced the impression that Byron was no mere armchair visionary or polemicist, but a careful, thoughtful, observer who had been to the places he wrote about and who knew what he was talking about.
24    [ed.: 'firman', a letter of permission from the Turkish authorities]
25    Note to Canto II, line 6; *CPW* II, 189–90.

At this moment [...], besides what has been already deposited in London, an Hydriot vessel is in the Piraeus to receive every portable relic. Thus, as I heard a young Greek observe in common with many of his countrymen—for, lost as they are, they yet feel on this occasion—thus may Lord Elgin boast of having ruined Athens. An Italian painter of the first eminence, named Lusieri, is the agent of devastation; and, like the Greek *finder* of Verres in Sicily, who followed the same profession, he has proved the able instrument of plunder. Between this artist and the French Consul Fauvel, who wishes to rescue the remains for his own government, there is now a violent dispute concerning a car employed in their conveyance, the wheel of which—I wish they were both broken upon it—has been locked up by the Consul, and Lusieri has laid his complaint before the Waywode.[26] Lord Elgin has been extremely happy in his choice of Signor Lusieri. During a residence of ten years in Athens, he never had the curiosity to proceed as far as Sunium, till he accompanied us in our second excursion. However, his works, as far as they go, are most beautiful; but they are almost all unfinished.[27]

*Childe Harold's Pilgrimage* is, among much else, a political poem. In the verse part Byron's view is an uncompromising reassertion of the philhellenic myth. Ignoring two thousand years of intervening history, Byron asserts an identity between the Modern Greeks of the nineteenth century and their putative ancestors, the Ancient Greeks of the classical age. The Modern Greeks are a degenerate enslaved nation who will only be freed when they begin to imitate their ancestors and start a violent revolution. The rich Westerners coming to visit the birthplace of civilization invariably drew melancholy comparisons between the glories of ancient Greece and her modern degradation. It was a pleasing antithesis especially as they and their readers were in no doubt that their own countries now represented the acme of modern civilization.

> And lo! he comes, the modern son of Greece,
> The shame of Athens: mark him how he bears
> A look o'eraw'd and moulded to the stamp
> Of servitude.[28]

---

26  [ed.: 'Waywode', Turkish governor of Athens]
27  Note to Canto II, line 101; *CPW* II, 190–91.
28  William Haygarth, *Greece, A Poem in Three Parts* (London: W. Bulmer & Co, 1814), Part II, lines 222 ff., https://www.google.co.uk/books/edition/Greece/_oJOAQAAMAAJ?hl=en&gbpv=1

So wrote William Haygarth and most of the travellers agreed with him. That the Greeks were a thoroughly contemptible race was, it was said, the only point on which Fauvel and Lusieri were agreed.[29] Byron alone was of a different opinion. In his notes to *Childe Harold* he declared:

> They are so unused to kindness that when they occasionally meet with it they look upon it with suspicion, as a dog often beaten snaps at your fingers if you attempt to caress him. 'They are ungrateful, notoriously, abominably ungrateful!'—this is the general cry. Now, in the name of Nemesis! for what are they to be grateful? Where is the human being that ever conferred a benefit on Greek or Greeks? They are to be grateful to the Turks for their fetters, and the Franks for their broken promises and lying counsels: they are to be grateful to the artist who engraves their ruins, and to the antiquary who carries them away; to the traveller whose janissary flogs them, and to the scribbler whose journal abuses them! This is the amount of their obligations to foreigners.[30]

In the prose notes Byron offers an alternative, even a contradictory, discourse, to the rhetoric of the verse. The Greeks will never be independent, he notes, and in any case it is nonsense to discuss the problems of contemporary Greece in terms of their putative ancestors. That is like discussing the future of Peru in terms of the Incas.

As a guide to the contemporary political situation in Greece, the notes to *Childe Harold* are more reliable than the verse. And it was by no means obvious that the future of a land inhabited for hundreds of years by peoples of different traditions and religions in conditions of social harmony lay in driving out the minorities and trying to establish a homogeneous nation state. Capodistria, the most eminent Greek of the time, put his faith in a gradualist approach, relying on the spread of education to liberalize the institutions of the Ottoman state. Others looked forward to the day, which did not seem far distant, when the Greeks would supersede the Turks as the dominant group within the Ottoman empire, would gradually take over more and more of the positions of power, and establish a new Byzantium. The educated Greek classes who, apart from a large diaspora in western Europe, mostly lived in Constantinople were strong upholders of the Ottoman system

---

29   *Childe Harold's Pilgrimage*, Canto II, 'Papers referred to by Note [to Stanza 73]'; *CPW* II, 201.

30   *CPW* II, 201.

in which they filled many positions of power and wealth.[31] Few of the Greeks living in the territory of present-day Greece shared the views set out in the verse part of *Childe Harold's Pilgrimage*, and would not have understood his allusions. They did not, in Elgin and Byron's time, think of themselves in nationalist terms. They were not Hellenes, but the Orthodox Christian inhabitants of a large multicultural empire. When Western travellers heard stories about the great men and women of ancient times, they thought they had picked up a genuine continuous tradition, but in most cases, it is likely that they were repeating back stories derived from previous travellers.[32]

Even before the custom began of leaving out the prose notes, it was the message of the verse which readers wanted to hear. In the decades after 1812 the fame and influence of Byron's Grecian poems helped to consolidate and strengthen the philhellenic fallacy first in Europe, and soon, increasingly, in Greece itself. And from the beginning the Parthenon became an integral part of the construction of the Modern Greek sense of national identity, a visible and tangible manifestation of the continuity which the myth required and asserted.

Some weeks before *Childe Harold's Pilgrimage* was due to be published Byron received a letter from Edward Daniel Clarke, the Cambridge professor who had quarrelled with Carlyle and Hunt[33] in the Troad in 1801 and had subsequently witnessed the taking down of the first sculptures from the Parthenon. Clarke reported that Lord Aberdeen wished to propose Byron for membership of the Athenian Club, a club of rich young men who had visited Athens, almost an offshoot of the dilettanti.

The letter put Byron in a dilemma. On the one hand, he seems to have been genuinely flattered to be invited. On the other, he was afraid

---

31 See, for example, C. M. Woodhouse, *Capodistria: The Founder of Greek Independence* (New York: Oxford University Press, 1973) and the documents in *The Movement for Greek Independence, 1770–1821*, ed. and trans. by Richard Clogg (London: Macmillan, 1976).

32 In the 1970s, a friend of mine doing research on the life of Lawrence of Arabia was taken to meet an old Bedouin who spoke confidently about Lawrence whom he gave every appearance of having known personally. It turned out that his information was derived from seeing the film.

33 [ed.: Joseph Dacre Carlyle (1758–1804) and Philip Hunt (1772–1838), both Anglican priests, on Lord's Elgin's staff.]

of how the Athenian Club would receive the attacks on Lord Elgin in his forthcoming poem. In his reply to Clarke, Byron remarked:

> In the notes to a thing of mine now passing through the press there is some notice taken of an agent of Ld. A's in the Levant, *Grossius* by name, & a few remarks on Ld. Elgin, Lusieri & and their pursuits, which may render the writer not very acceptable to a zealous Antiquarian.—Ld. A's is not mentioned or alluded to in any manner personally disrespectful, but Ld. Elgin is spoken of according to the writer's decided opinion of *him* and *his* [...] Truth is I am sadly deficient in gusto and have little of the antique spirit except a wish to immolate Ld. Elgin to Minerva and Nemesis.[34]

Lord Aberdeen was prepared to overlook the remarks on antiquarians but Byron did not join the Athenian Club. The exchange of correspondence with Clarke did, however, reveal that he too was an old enemy of Lord Elgin and an alliance directed against Elgin's reputation grew up between the two men. In writing to congratulate Byron on the publication of *Childe Harold's Pilgrimage*, Clarke told him the story of the damage caused to the Parthenon cornice when the first metope was taken down and of how the Disdar[35] had wept when he saw it. Byron gratefully incorporated the story with due acknowledgement in the notes to subsequent editions of his poem.[36] Clarke, in his turn, asked permission to quote from *Childe Harold's Pilgrimage* in the enormous book of *Travels* on which he was then engaged and obtained Byron's thanks for 'preserving my relics embalmed in your own spices &—ensuring me readers to whom I could not otherwise have aspired'.[37]

In his huge multi-volume *Travels in Various Countries of Europe, Asia and Africa* Clarke attacked Elgin mercilessly for 'want of taste and utter

---

34   Byron to Clarke, 19 January 1812, *BLJ* II, 156. Marchand reads 'Grossius', but, having looked again at the manuscript, British Library Egerton MS 2869, fol. 7, I believe that the true reading is 'Gropius'. Georg Gropius was Aberdeen's agent. Byron frequently made jokes on names but the manuscript suggests no such intention here. In *Childe Harold's Pilgrimage*, Canto II, note to line 101, Byron says that Aberdeen completely disowned Gropius' collecting activities (*CPW* II, 191). It is clear, however, from a letter of Hamilton to Elgin (May 1809, Elgin Papers) that Aberdeen at that time was laying claim to the vases collected by Gropius. The occasion of Byron's apology to Aberdeen is described in British Library Add. MS 43230, fol. 114.

35   [ed.: 'Disdar', warden of a castle or fort, in this case, of the Acropolis]

36   In all editions after the first.

37   Letter to Clarke, 15 December 1813; *BLJ* III, 199.

barbarism'.[38] The Parthenon sculptures removed from their original setting, he said, lost all their excellence. Elgin was compared to 'another nobleman who being delighted at a Puppet Show, bought Punch and was chagrined to find when he carried him home, that the figure had lost all its humour'.[39] Clarke's narrative (which described proudly the numerous removals of antiquities which he himself had accomplished and includes several views drawn by Lusieri and the Calmuck which had improperly come into his possession) provides ample confirmation of Elgin's view that the Parthenon was being quickly destroyed and that the Turks were incapable of preventing it even if they had wished. The British public knew nothing of what lay behind the scenes. To them it seemed simply that the opinions of the passionate poet were being confirmed by the painstaking researches of the scholar.

Byron was being a little disingenuous in telling Clarke that it was only Elgin that he wished to attack. At a late stage before publication the manuscript of *Childe Harold's Pilgrimage* contained the following lines:

> Come then, ye classic Thieves of each degree,
> Dark Hamilton and sullen Aberdeen,
> Come pilfer all the Pilgrim loves to see,
> All that yet consecrates the fading scene—
> Ah! better were it ye had never been,
> Nor ye, nor Elgin, nor that lesser wight,
> The victim sad of vase-collecting spleen,
> House-furnisher withal, one Thomas hight,
> Than ye should bear one stone from wronged Athena's sight.[40]

Dark Hamilton is probably Sir William Hamilton, who had bought many antiquities while ambassador in Naples, although it was William Richard Hamilton, Elgin's private secretary, who had been involved in the Elgin collecting. Lord Aberdeen too had removed pieces of sculpture from the Parthenon and fully deserved the charge of pilfering. 'One Thomas hight' is Thomas Hope, another prominent member of the Dilettanti, author of a book on ancient furniture, who had obtained a sculptured

38    Edward Daniel Clarke, *Travels in Various Countries of Europe, Asia and Africa*, 6 vols (London: Printed for T. Cadell and W. Davies, 1810–23), Part II, section 2, 484, https://wellcomecollection.org/works/ddmjahws/items

39    Clarke, *Travels*, II, 2, 485.

40    British Library Egerton MS 2027; *CPW* II, 48.

fragment from Athens several years before which he exhibited in his London house as a fragment of the Parthenon.[41]

In another rejected stanza Byron suggests:

> Or will the gentle Dilettanti crew
> New delegate the task to digging Gell

and comments 'According to Lusieri's account he (Gell) began digging most furiously without a firman but before the resurrection of a single sauce-pan the Painter [Lusieri] countermined and the Waywode countermanded and sent him back to bookmaking'.[42]

In the notes to *Childe Harold's Pilgrimage* as it was published Lord Aberdeen is not mentioned by name. He is 'Lord—' exempt from even the usual partial identification of asterisks. He is, compared with Elgin, 'another noble Lord [who] has done better, because he has done less'.[43] Georg Gropius, who acted as Lord Aberdeen's agent in collecting antiquities although he pretended to be only a painter, quarrelled with Lusieri over the ownership of some vases, each claiming them for his master. In the early editions of *Childe Harold's Pilgrimage*, Byron tells a story that Lusieri challenged Gropius to a duel and asked Byron to arbitrate.[44] In later editions Byron withdrew even these heavily veiled criticisms of Lord Aberdeen in an unnecessarily profuse apology.

Byron at one time considered making a reference to Elgin's nose and to his wife. A rejected passage declared:

> Albion! I would not see thee thus adorned
> With gains thy generous spirit should have scorned,
> From Man distinguished by some monstrous sign,
> Like Attila the Hun was surely horned
> Who wrought this ravage amid works divine
> Oh that Minerva's voice lent its keen aid to mine.[45]

---

41   *Ancient Marbles in Great Britain*, described by Adolf Michaelis, trans. by
     C. A. M. Fennell (Cambridge: Cambridge University Press, 1882), p. 285, https://
     archive.org/details/ancientmarblesin00michuoft.

42   Egerton MS 2027; *Manuscripts of the Younger Romantics VI: Childe Harold's
     Pilgrimage*, ed. by David V. Erdman with the assistance of David Worrall (New
     York: Garland, 1991), p. 109.

43   *Childe Harold's Pilgrimage*, Canto II, note to line 101; *CPW* II, 191.

44   Ibid.

45   Egerton MS 2027; *CPW* II, 48.

Besides Clarke, more and more travellers returning from Greece took up their pens and, since the war had put a stop to the Grand Tour of Italy, more travellers found their way to Greece in the early part of the nineteenth century than ever before. Almost without exception they had something disparaging to say of Elgin although equally they were all full of praise for Lusieri. F. S N. Douglas, who wrote a book comparing the Ancient and Modern Greeks, while admitting most of Elgin's arguments in the *Memorandum*, concluded:

> It appears to me a very flagrant piece of injustice to deprive a helpless and friendly nation of any possession of value to them [...] I wonder at the boldness of the hand that could venture to remove what Phidias had placed under the inspection of Pericles.[46]

Edward Dodwell, himself a despoiler of the Parthenon, wrote of Elgin's 'insensate barbarism' and of 'his devastating outrage which will never cease to be deplored'.[47] Thomas Hughes, another visitor to Athens, wrote of Elgin's 'wanton devastation' and 'avidity for plunder'.[48] J. C. Eustace in a popular *Classical Tour through Italy* condemned Elgin fiercely without having been to Athens and seen the circumstances there.[49] French travellers combined indignation at Elgin with regret that the marbles had not gone to the Louvre. Chateaubriand joined in the condemnation although, when he left Athens, he too had a piece of the Parthenon in his pocket.[50]

---

46  F. S. N. Douglas, *An Essay on Certain Points of Resemblance between the Ancient and Modern Greeks* (London: John Murray, 1813), p. 89, https://archive.org/details/anessayoncertai00dougoog

47  Edward Dodwell, *A Classical and Topographical Tour through Greece, during the years 1801, 1805, and 1806*, 2 vols (London: Rodwell and Martin, 1819), I, 324, 322, https://www.google.co.uk/books/edition/A_Classical_and_Topographical_Tour_Throu/sgkXAAAAYAAJ?hl=en&gbpv=1

48  T. S. Hughes, *Travels in Sicily, Greece and Albania*, 2 vols (London: J. Mawman, 1820), I, 261, https://archive.org/details/travelsinsicily01hughgoog/page/n5/mode/2up

49  J. C. Eustace, *A Tour through Italy*, 2 vols (London: J. Mawman, 1813), II, 20. Notes to pp. 192–94, https://archive.org/details/classicaltouritaly03eust

50  Especially F. C. H. L. Pouqueville, *Voyage dans la Grèce*, 5 vols (Paris: Firmin Didot, Père et Fils, 1820–21), IV, 36, 74, https://gallica.bnf.fr/ark:/12148/bpt6k97401533.image; J. L. S. Bartholdy, *Voyage en Grèce* (Paris: Dentu, 1807), p. 45, https://www.google.co.uk/books/edition/Voyage_en_Gr%C3%A8ce_1803_04/TZ8wAAAAYAAJ?hl=en&gbpv=1; and Louis, Comte de Forbin, *Voyage dans le Levant en 1817 et 1818*, 2 vols, 2nd edn (Paris: Delaunay, 1819), II, https://www.

During the centuries when the Parthenon was a Christian church, the names of the bishops of Athens were inscribed on one of the columns. In 1802, in a new form of cultural appropriation, the names Elgin and Mary Elgin with the date of their visit were carved deeply and clearly about half-way up one of the columns of the Parthenon in a place which Hunt had specially reserved in May 1801.[51] Elgin's name was soon deliberately erased but that of Mary Elgin could still be read in 1826.[52] Byron's name could be seen carved on several monuments which he had visited, at Sounion, in the quarry at Pentelikon, on the wall of the monastery at Delphi, on the Monument of Lysicrates and hidden in one of the capitals of the Erechtheion.[53]

On one of the surviving original Caryatids some wit from the West wrote 'Opus Phidiae' (the work of Phidias). On the crude brick pillar substituted for the Caryatid removed by Elgin's agents, he wrote 'Opus Elgin' (the work of Elgin).[54] Another traveller, familiar with the ancient Greek convention of signing works of art, wrote, in Greek, 'Elgin Made Me'.[55] A better joke could be seen carved on a wall inside the Erechtheion. There some donnish wit, recalling the story that even Alaric and his Visigoths had respected the monuments of Athens, wrote the Latin rhyme 'Quod non fecerunt Goti, hoc fecerunt Scoti' ('What was not done by the Goths was done by the Scots').[56] Travelling gentlemen would have recognized the echo of the older tag about the Popes of Rome who used bronze from the Pantheon in the building

google.co.uk/books/edition/Voyage_dans_le_Levant_en_1817_et_1818/cFY9AAA
AcAAJ?hl=en&gbpv=1&printsec=frontcover

51    François-René, vicomte de Chateaubriand, *Travels to Jerusalem and the Holy Land, through Egypt*, 2 vols, 3rd edn, trans. by Frederic Shoberl (London: H. Colburn, 1835), I, 187, https://archive.org/details/travelstojerusal02chat/page/n5/mode/2up

52    Hunt to Elgin, 22 May 1801, Elgin Papers.

53    William Black, *Narratives of Cruises in the Mediterranean* (Edinburgh: Oliver and Boyd, 1900), p. 295. Black gives the date 1806, which is clearly impossible, https://wellcomecollection.org/works/b69gt278/items

54    See C. W. J. Eliot, 'Lord Byron, Early Travelers, and the Monastery at Delphi', *American Journal of Archaeology*, 71.3 (1967), 283–91. For the name on the Monument of Lysicrates and the Erechtheion, not, as far as I know, found during the recent careful examination connected with the restorations, see N. Parker Willis, *Summer Cruise in the Mediterranean* (London: T. Nelson and Sons, 1853), pp.145 and 148, https://www.gutenberg.org/ebooks/48264

55    Forbin, *Voyage dans le Levant*, II.

56    Dodwell, *Classical Tour*, I, 353, and *Quarterly Review* (May 1820).

of St Peter's. 'Quod non fecerunt barbari, fecerunt Barberini' ('What barbarians did not do, was done by Barberini'). These jibes, clearly intended to impress other travellers and not the Greeks or Turks, were gleefully recounted by travellers and taken up by the newspapers and literary reviews at home. Within a few years the stories current among the foreign colony in Athens were so confused that Elgin was soon being blamed for actions he never committed.[57] Indignation at the Turks waned in proportion.

The most bitter attack of all was *The Curse of Minerva* by Lord Byron. Like the first part of *Childe Harold's Pilgrimage* some of it was composed when Byron was in Athens, but it appears to have been mostly written on his return to England.[58] Originally it was intended that the two poems should be published together in 1812 along with some other of Byron's satires. At the last moment, however, owing to the intervention of one of Elgin's friends, Byron decided not to publish the *Curse* and the full version did not appear under his name until some years later.[59]

Byron had not the heart to suppress it entirely.[60] In 1812 a few copies were printed and sent to Byron's friends. To Clarke, for instance, in thanks for the story about the Disdar, Byron wrote 'I have printed 8 copies of a certain thing, one of which shall be yours'.[61] Samuel Rogers had another, and no doubt many people had an opportunity of reading it.[62] In 1815 a pirated copy, much mutilated, appeared in the *New*

57    John Cam Hobhouse, *A Journey through Albania and other provinces of Turkey in Europe and Asia, to Constantinople, during the years 1809 and 1810* (London: James Cawthorne, 1813), p. 345, https://www.google.co.uk/books/edition/A_Journey_Through_Albania_and_Other_Prov/8nfVAAAAMAAJ?hl=en&gbpv=1. Many other references.

58    A. H. Smith, 'Lord Elgin and His Collection', *The Journal of Hellenic Studies*, 36 (1916), 163–372 (220), quoting William Turner, *Journal of a Tour in the Levant*, 3 vols (London: John Murray, 1820), I, 347, https://www.google.co.uk/books/edition/Journal_of_a_Tour_in_the_Levant/dCoNAAAAYAAJ?hl=en&gbpv=1.

59    *CPW* I, 320–30.

60    The suggestion in Moore's *Byron*, Chapter 55, that Byron's decision was aided by a 'friendly remonstrance from Lord Elgin or some of his connection' is confirmed by a reference in the Journal of Edward Everett. Everett met Byron on 18 June 1815 shortly after Elgin's Petition to Parliament was debated. 'I asked him,' he wrote, 'whether his poem which he speaks of as "printed but not published" in the notes to the *Corsair*, would ever be given to the World. Oh No! he replied it was a satire upon Lord Elgin, which a particular friend of each had begged him to suppress.'

61    Byron to Clarke, 27 May 1812. British Library, Egerton MS 2869, fol. 10; *BLJ* II, 178.

62    Rogers's copy is in the British Library. It seems likely that many more than eight copies were printed.

*Monthly Magazine* and other versions began to circulate some months later.[63] Although Byron attempted to disown the pirated versions, his authorship was clear.[64] Another poem called *The Parthenon* published by James and Horace Smith in 1813 bears evidence of having been paraphrased from *The Curse of Minerva*.[65]

*The Curse of Minerva* begins with a beautiful descriptive passage on the evening in Greece which Byron used again in *The Corsair*. The poet (as in *Childe Harold's Pilgrimage*) sits alone and friendless within the walls of the ruined Parthenon when suddenly Minerva herself appears. She is hardly recognizable. Her aegis holds no terrors, her armour is dented, and her lance is broken.

> 'Mortal!'('twas thus she spake) 'that blush of shame
> Proclaims thee Briton, once a noble name;
> First of the mighty, foremost of the free,
> Now honoured *less* by all, and *least* by me:
> Chief of thy foes shall Pallas still be found—
> Seek'st thou the cause of loathing?—look around.
> Lo! here, despite of war and wasting fire,
> I saw successive tyrannies expire.
> 'Scaped from the ravage of the Turk and Goth,
> Thy country sends a spoiler worse than both.
> Survey this vacant, violated fane;
> Recount the relics torn that yet remain:
> *These* Cecrops placed, *this* Pericles adorn'd.
> *That* Adrian rear'd when drooping Science mourn'd.'[66]

Byron claimed in a footnote that he was referring to the Temple of Olympian Zeus built by Hadrian, not here subscribing to the Payne Knight view that the Parthenon sculptures were Hadrianic. The poem continues:

---

63  *New Monthly Magazine*, April 1815, 'The Malediction of Minerva'. This version is very corrupt and bears the signs of having passed through several manuscript versions before reaching the printer. *The Curse of Minerva*, in its abbreviated form, also appeared in editions sold by the Paris pirate publisher Galignani.

64  A month after 'The Malediction of Minerva' was published in the *New Monthly Magazine* a correspondent had pointed out that the author was Byron, *New Monthly Magazine*, September 1815. Other versions of *The Curse* were published in London in 1816, 1818, and 1819. Full versions under Byron's name were published in the United States in 1815 and 1816.

65  [James and Horace Smith], *Horace in London* (1813), ode xv, 'The Parthenon'.

66  *Curse of Minerva*, lines 89–102; *CPW* I, 323.

'What more I owe let Gratitude attest—
Know Alaric and Elgin did the rest.
That all may learn from whence the plunderer came
The insulted wall sustains his hated name:
For Elgin's fame thus grateful Pallas pleads,
Below, his name; above behold his deeds!
Be ever hail'd with equal honour here
The Gothic monarch and the Pictish peer:
Arms gave the first his right, the last had none,
But basely stole what less barbarians won.
So when the Lion quits his fell repast
Next prowls the Wolf, the filthy Jackal last:
Flesh, limbs and blood the former make their own,
The last poor brute securely gnaws the bone.'

Minerva then observes that another goddess has helped to avenge her:

'Yet still the Gods are just, and crimes are crost:
See here what Elgin won, and what he lost!
Another name with *his* pollutes my shrine:
Behold where Dian's beams disdain to shine!
Some retribution still might Pallas claim,
When Venus half aveng'd Minerva's shame.'[67]

To those in the know, Elgin's syphilis, his cuckolding, and his divorce
are a punishment for his sacrilege.

To this outburst from Minerva the poet dares to make some reply.
Do not blame England for this terrible deed, he says. England disowns
him, the plunderer was a Scot. Just as Boeotia was the uncivilized part
of Greece, so Scotland is the uncivilized part of Britain:

'And well I know within that bastard land
Hath Wisdom's goddess never held command:
A barren soil where Nature's germs confin'd
To stern sterility can stint the mind,
Whose thistle well betrays the niggard earth,
Emblem of all to whom the land gives birth;
Each genial influence nurtur'd to resist,
A land of meanness, sophistry and mist.
Each breeze from foggy mount and marshy plain
Dilutes with drivel every drizzly brain,
Till burst at length each watery head o'erflows,

---

67   *Curse of Minerva*, lines 103–22; *CPW* I, 323–34.

> Foul as their soil and frigid as their snows;
> Then thousand schemes of petulance and pride
> Dispatch her scheming children far and wide,
> Some East, some West, some every where but North,
> In quest of lawless gain they issue forth.
> And thus, accursed be the day and year!
> She sent a Pict to play the felon here.'[68]

It was necessary for the argument that Elgin's Scottishness should be stressed. But Byron was conscious of his own Scottish origins, and obviously did not want to be included in his own condemnation. His solution was very neat and contains one of the few hints of humour in the poem. Just as Boeotia managed to produce a Pindar, he said, so there was hope for a few Scotsmen, 'the letter'd and the brave', provided they were prepared to shake off the sordid dust of their native land.

Minerva curses not only Elgin but his children. The only surviving son, Byron knew, was mentally retarded. As for his other children, from what had been said about Lady Elgin at the divorce trial, could Elgin be sure that he was really their father?

> 'First on the head of him who did this deed
> My curse shall light, on him and all his seed:
> Without one spark of intellectual fire,
> Be all the sons as senseless as the sire:
> If one with wit the parent brood disgrace,
> Believe him bastard of a brighter race:
> Still with his hireling artists let him prate,
> And Folly's praise repay for Wisdom's hate;
> Long of their Patron's gusto let them tell,
> Whose noblest, *native* gusto is—to sell:
> To sell, and make, may Shame record the day,
> The State receiver of his pilfer'd prey:
> Meanwhile, the flattering, feeble dotard West,
> Europe's worst dauber, and poor Britain's best,
> With palsied hand shall turn each model o'er,
> And own himself an infant of fourscore:
> Be all the bruisers cull'd from all St. Giles,
> That art and nature may compare their styles;
> While brawny brutes in stupid wonder stare,
> And marvel at his lordship's "stone shop" there.'[69]

---

68   *Curse of Minerva*, lines 131–48; *CPW* I, 324–35.
69   *Curse of Minerva*, lines 163–82; *CPW* I, 325–36.

After some amusing remarks about the embarrassment of the young ladies of London at seeing such huge naked manly statues Minerva pronounces her curse. Lord Elgin, like Eratostratus who set fire to the Temple of Diana at Ephesus, will be for ever hated: 'loath'd in life, nor pardon'd in the dust.' Vengeance will pursue him far beyond the grave 'In many a branding page and burning line'.[70]

Elgin's deed is so terrible that it is not enough that he alone should be punished. Britain herself must suffer the penalty. The terrible war on which she has embarked will soon destroy her. In the Baltic and the Peninsula she will be defeated. In the East the Indians will 'shake her tyrant empire to its base'. At home Minerva will strike. Trade will languish, famine break out, the Government become powerless. The country itself will be invaded and ravaged. And, says Minerva, no one will be sorry. It is too late. The country has brought all this upon herself.

*Childe Harold's Pilgrimage* and *The Curse of Minerva* have coloured the world's view of Lord Elgin's activities ever since they first appeared. And it is no criticism of a satirist to say that he gives only one side of an argument. On the other hand, the indignation of satirists which appears to be spontaneous and heart-felt is often little more than a literary exercise, an attempt to recapture the spirit of Juvenal and of Pope. When Byron was in Athens John Galt was writing voluminously both in prose and verse. As his letters show, Galt clearly recognized that the antiquities of Greece were being quickly destroyed by the travellers and by the Turks and that if Elgin had not removed the Parthenon marbles the French certainly would.[71] Nor was he averse from acquiring them himself if he had had the chance.[72] While he was staying at the Capuchin Convent, however, Galt knocked out a satire on Lord Elgin which he called the *Atheniad*.[73] He showed this to Byron, who kept the manuscript for several weeks before returning it by way of Hobhouse. On his return to England Galt intended to publish his poem but, like Byron, he was

---

70   *Curse of Minerva*, lines 199, 204; CPW I, 327.

71   John Galt, *Letters from the Levant* (London: T. Cadell and W. Davies, 1813), p. 112, letter dated 1 March 1810, https://www.google.co.uk/books/edition/Letters_from_the_Levant/7A4IAAAAQAAJ?hl=en&gbpv=1.

72   John Galt, *Autobiography* (London: Cochrane and M'Crone, 1833), Chapter 7.

73   An edited version of the *Atheniad* was published in Galt, *Autobiography*. Another version appeared many years earlier in the *Monthly Magazine*, 49 (1820).

dissuaded by one of Elgin's friends, in this case Hamilton.[74] It was not published until 1820.

The *Atheniad* is an amateurish piece of mock heroics, good-humoured enough on the whole. Where the *Curse* becomes bitter against Lord Elgin, the *Atheniad* merely shows bad taste. It was clearly never intended to be more than a literary exercise. In Galt's satire, the gods of Olympus, dejected by the oppression of Greece, are consoled somewhat by the memory of the former glories of Athens and by the contemplation of her ruins. Then Fate takes a hand. Mercury is sent back to earth disguised as a man called 'Dontitos' (Don Tita Lusieri). 'Cadaverous, crafty, skilled in tints and lines, A lean Italian master of designs', Dontitos seeks out a nobleman called 'Brucides' (Lord Elgin) and tells him he will be famous if only he will rescue the Parthenon sculptures from the Turks. Brucides falls for this trap and sets to work.

> With ready gold he calls men, carts, and cords,
> Cords, carts and men, rise at the baited words.
> The ropes asunder rive the wedded stone,
> The mortals labour and the axles groan,
> Hymettus echoes to the tumbling fane,
> And shook th' Acropolis—shakes all the plain.[75]

Suddenly the gods of Olympus realize what is happening and one by one they take their revenge. First Neptune conjures up a storm and sinks Brucides' vessel at Cythera. Minerva inspires Brucides with delirious fancies so that his diplomatic dispatches are filled with talk of 'basso-relievos' and 'marble blocks' instead of military and political affairs— Brucides at once loses his ambassadorship. On the way home, however, Brucides makes a partial recovery. He lingers in Italy and France and 'still has sprightly pleasures left'. But Minerva soon has the better of him. She drives to Paris in her golden chariot and disguising herself as

---

74   In a letter to Elgin on 17 September 1811 Hamilton wrote: 'I saw Mr. Hume a few days ago who called to give me the satisfactory intelligence that M. Gant [*sic*] had given up all idea of bringing to light the production of his Muse, and that the absence of Lord Biron [*sic*] had given him time to reflect on the improper tendency of his former intentions', Elgin Papers. Hamilton's misspelling of the names of Galt and Byron shows how little known both men were at the time.

75   [John Galt], 'The Atheniad; Or, The Rape of the Parthenon', *Monthly Magazine* 49.336 (1 February, 1820), https://archive.org/stream/sim_monthly-magazine_1820-02-01_49_336/sim_monthly-magazine_1820-02-01_49_336_djvu.txt

Talleyrand, she persuades Napoleon to arrest all the British in France and so to possess Brucides 'a prize more precious than the Greeks of old, From Ilion stole'.

Meanwhile Mars too is taking his revenge. In order to effect the transfer of a very useful cart from 'Fouvelle' (Fauvel) to Dontitos he stirs up wars in Egypt, Russia, and Spain, and finally, in a delightful piece of bathos, causes a conflict in Athens over the wheel of this cart, which by 1810 had changed hands between Fauvel and Lusieri at least four times. Next Venus in her turn takes her revenge on Brucides, but the poet is reluctant to speak of it—he is forbidden by Juno. Those in the know would detect the usual references to syphilis and cuckoldry. Cupid's revenge is to thrust a flaming torch into Elgin's face disfiguring him to look like a noseless antique bust. And finally Apollo vents his wrath by inspiring John Galt to record these great events 'in epic strains'.

> Thus wrought the gods in old Athenia's cause,
> Avenged their fanes, and will'd the world's applause.

*The Curse of Minerva* clearly owes some of its ideas to the *Atheniad* although its whole tone is different and Galt was never able to persuade Byron to acknowledge any debt.[76] Most probably it was the idea itself that Galt inspired. Perhaps Byron on reading Galt's literary effort, decided that he could do much better than his tedious companion and dashed off the *Curse*. It may be a literary extravaganza. *Childe Harold's Pilgrimage*, too, undoubtedly owes much to its literary predecessors. Its main theme—that of a reborn Greece rising against the Turks—was far from new when Byron wrote: it was already a well-known literary genre.[77] A long anonymous poem on this theme—*A Letter from Athens addressed to a Friend in England*—appeared almost simultaneously with the first two cantos of *Childe Harold's Pilgrimage*.[78] Another—William Haygarth's *Greece*—was actually being written when Byron was in Athens and he knew and liked its author. All three poems show similarities of idea if not

---

76  John Galt, *Life of Byron* (London: Henry Colburn and Richard Bentley, 1830), p. 183, https://www.google.co.uk/books/edition/The_Life_of_Lord_Byron/ guwyAQAAMAAJ?hl=en&gbpv=1

77  For a discussion of this point see Terence Spencer, *Fair Greece, Sad Relic*, pp. 247 ff., and St Clair, *That Greece Might Still Be Free*, early chapters.

78  Kelsall. Name of the author from Spencer, *Fire Greece, Sad Relic*, p. 279.

of style. Haygarth's *Greece* also has a few resemblances in construction to *The Curse of Minerva*.

Is then Byron's indignation against Elgin purely literary? Was he being no more serious in attacking Elgin than he was in his satire against the *English Bards and Scotch Reviewers*, much of whose unfairness he later regretted? Was his main objection Elgin's 'robbery of Athens to instruct the English in sculpture'.[79] Or was there something about Elgin personally which roused his anger, his Scottishness, for example, or his Toryism, or his apparently typical British contempt for foreigners? The cruelty of *The Curse of Minerva* is unusually personal. Possibly the answer lies in Byron's sheer perverseness, his wish to be different from the careful moderation of Hobhouse and Galt. Writing of *Childe Harold's Pilgrimage* in September 1811, some months before it was published, he declared boldly that he had been forced into the attack by the contemptuous review of his first poems which had appeared in the *Edinburgh Review*:

> I have attacked De Pauw, Thornton, Lord Elgin, Spain, Portugal, the *Edinburgh Review*, travellers, Painters, Antiquarians, and others, so you see what a dish of Sour Crout Controversy I shall prepare for myself. It would not answer for me to give way now; as I was forced into bitterness at the beginning, I will go through to the last. *Vae Victis!* If I fall I shall fall gloriously, fighting against a host.[80]

Byron's attack fell on a man who was already almost broken by his misfortunes. Lord Elgin, trying desperately to restore his finances in his Scottish retreat, was strangely silent. The world's reception of *Childe Harold's Pilgrimage* coming so soon after his rebuff from Spencer Perceval[81] seemed merely another in the long series of misfortunes to which he was now almost accustomed. After *Childe Harold's Pilgrimage* it seemed to Elgin that every time he opened the *Edinburgh* or the *Quarterly Review*, yet another book of travels had been published with its inevitable sneers

---

79   Byron, *A Letter to * *** [John Murray] on the Rev. W. L. Bowles's Strictures on the Life and Writings of Pope* (London: John Murray, 1821), p. 25.

80   Byron to Hodgson, 25 September 1811; *BLJ* II, 106. De Pauw and Thornton were authors of books contemptuous of the Modern Greeks.

81   [ed.: In a previous chapter, St Clair described the snub administered by the Prime Minister, Spencer Perceval, to Elgin's proposal that he be awarded a peerage: 'To a Scotch peer, [...] nothing could be so desirable as a British peerage' (*Lord Elgin*, pp. 177–78).]

and accusations. What could be the meaning of it all? What had he done to deserve such treatment? He had only done what men of his class had been doing for over a hundred years, the exception being that his interest in antiquities had been so genuine that it had ruined him. There must be some explanation, Elgin felt. The world could not be so unjust without some cause.

Who could the arch conspirator be? Could it be his hated neighbour Robert Ferguson of Raith, the man who had run away with his wife and whom he had successfully sued for £10,000? Possibly. Ferguson, who sat in Parliament as a Whig, might have persuaded his friends in those days of increasing political bitterness to attack a prominent Tory.[82] Could it be Clarke? His hatred of Elgin seemed to be unlimited, despite the many kindnesses he had accepted at Constantinople. This too was a possibility, although it was unlikely that a mere Cambridge don could exert so much influence.

But there was a man who held his grudge against Elgin more deeply than either of these. John Spencer Smith could not forget the disgrace of being superseded by Elgin as minister in Turkey and then of being dismissed for incompetence and disobedience. He could not forget too that the accusations which Napoleon had levelled against Elgin in 1804 of mistreating the French in Constantinople had subsequently been transferred by the French government to himself; and that, partly as a consequence, he was bundled out of his last diplomatic appointment in Württemberg. Here, Elgin suspected, was his conspirator. Spencer Smith's tongue was active against him in England and the merchants of the Levant Company were maligning him to travellers, English and French in Greece and Constantinople. The Levant Company had an interest in preventing any more ambassadors extraordinary being appointed to Constantinople to break their precarious monopoly.

---

82   This seems to have been Hamilton's explanation to Haydon, *The Diary of Benjamin Robert Haydon*, ed. by Willard Bissell Pope, 5 vols (Cambridge, MA: Harvard University Press, 1963), IV, 594: 'October 27, 1839. Spent the greater part of the day with Hamilton—a delightful one. He let me into the secret of the opposition of Lord Elgin at the time. He said Lady Elgin's Friends who were Tories (the Manners) & Ferguson's friends who were Whigs, were violent in their hatred of every thing he did, & made all that stir in opposition, backed by the jealousy of Connoisseurship.' Elgin's counsel accused Ferguson of deliberately attempting to misrepresent Elgin's public life in the divorce trial of December 1807. *Trial of R. J. Fergusson Esquire*, 9, and *Trial of R. Fergusson Esq.*, 8.

And had not Byron had an affair with Spencer Smith's wife in Malta on his way to Greece and commemorated the event in *Childe Harold's Pilgrimage*?[83]

Elgin was wrong in thinking his misfortunes were the result of a conspiracy. His detractors were too numerous and, for the most part, too independently minded to be so carefully disciplined. What looked like a conspiracy can be seen in retrospect to have been simply a conjuncture of events, the discovery of Ancient Greece and its triumph over Rome, the cultural shift in Western attitudes to works of art and literature known as romanticism, and the increasing power of western European notions of national identity and how it should be constructed, celebrated, and reinforced both in western Europe and, increasingly elsewhere.

---

83    Mrs Spencer Smith, the daughter of Baron Herbert, Austrian Ambassador to the Porte, had made a dramatic and romantic escape when the French entered Venice in 1806. This was related by the Marquis of Salvo in a book published in 1807. She is described in enthusiastic terms in Byron's letters. In *Childe Harold's Pilgrimage*, Canto II, 30, she is:

   Sweet Florence! could another ever share
   This wayward, loveless heart, it would be thine:
   But check'd by every tie, I may not dare
   To cast a worthless offering at thy shrine,
   Nor ask so dear a breast to feel one pang for mine. (*CPW* II, 54)

# 5. Byron, Stephens and the Future of Ruins[1]

## *Adrian Poole*

Byron has shaped the way we think about ruins.[2] In the early years of the nineteenth century he was writing about ruins of two different kinds: most immediately, the recent ruins created by years of war across a shattered Europe; and then the ancient ruins of Rome, Athens, Egypt. What was the relation between them? Not just of the distant past to the present—but also to the future? For ruins can be all too new, like the ruins created by the seismic upheavals of the previous twenty-five years across Europe, from 1789 to 1815 and beyond. What happens next, 'the day after'? A question all too urgent as we witness, from distances of varying safety and peril, the ruination being perpetrated as I write these words, in Ukraine and in Gaza, and elsewhere.

---

1     This is a revised version of an essay entitled 'Byron in Yucatán: War and Ruins', published in *The Influence and Legacy of Alexander von Humboldt in the Americas*, ed. by María Fernanda Valencia Suárez and Carolina Depetris (Mérida: UNAM, 2022), pp. 119–31. Reprinted by permission of the Universidad Nacional Autónoma de México.

2     See James Buzard, *The Beaten Track: European Tourism, Literature, and the Ways to 'Culture', 1800–1918* (Oxford: Clarendon Press, 1993), pp. 14–30. Andrew Elfenbein comments further that 'As James Buzard has documented, Byron's invention of his experience of European greatness as unique, privileged, and profoundly individual proved to be a boom to the Victorian tourist industry. Early Victorian guidebooks included substantial quotations from Byron's poems, especially *Childe Harold*, to guide tourists to develop themselves by copying Byron.' (*Byron and the Victorians* (Cambridge: Cambridge University Press, 1995), pp. 32–33). For discussion of Byron's complex investment in 'ruins', see William Keach, 'Romantic Writing and the Determinations of Cultural Property', *European Romantic Review*, 30.2 (2019), 223–37.

        https://doi.org/10.11647/OBP.0399.05

When the protagonist of Byron's poem *Childe Harold* (1812–18) encounters the ruins of Athens, his first question is 'Where are thy men of might? thy grand in soul?'[3] And Byron has an extensive, eloquent note to this effect:

> We can all feel, or imagine, the regret with which the ruins of cities, once the capitals of empires, are beheld; [...] But never did the littleness of man, and the vanity of his very best virtues, of patriotism to exalt, and of valour to defend his country, appear more conspicuous in the record of what Athens was, and the certainty of what she now is.[4]

The modern Greeks were degraded, so Byron (and others) considered, unworthy of the great ancestors who fought at Marathon and built the Parthenon.[5] But the fall was not complete. The contrast between past glory and present degradation was unfinished, an ongoing process to which the modern world was viciously contributing. Byron continues:

> This theatre of contention between mighty factions, of the struggles of orators, the exaltation and deposition of tyrants, the triumph and punishment of generals, is now become a scene of petty intrigue and perpetual disturbance, between the bickering agents of certain British nobility and gentry. 'The wild foxes, the owls and serpents in the ruins of Babylon', were surely less degrading than such inhabitants.[6]

So much may be conspicuous and certain, but what of the future? What can those ancient ruins tell us about what lies ahead? They can tell us that the past is not locked away; they can remind us that what is now past was once future. Look at the Parthenon: it has been 'a temple, a church, and a mosque'. It has been partly destroyed, rebuilt, re-purposed. It has served as a sacred place to different religions, and now it is suffering, as Byron sees it, a new kind of a violation, 'a triple sacrilege'.[7] Is this what the future holds, a world from which the idea of the sacred has been erased, its vestiges reduced to objects for sale? Perhaps. But who can know, for certain? The ancient Athenians could not have known that

---

3    *Childe Harold,* Canto II, 2, in *Byron: The Complete Poetical Works*, ed. by Jerome
     J. McGann, 7 vols (Oxford: Clarendon Press, 1980–93), II, 44. All subsequent
     references to Byron's poetry are to this edition, hereafter *CPW*.
4    *CPW* II, 189.
5    William St Clair makes the same points more extensively in the previous chapter.
6    Ibid.
7    *CPW* II, 190.

their temple would go on to serve as a church and a mosque, nor the even more ancient Babylonians that their great city would be razed to the ground, even as they had themselves razed Jerusalem. Those Old Testament images of wilderness to which Byron gestures—the wild foxes, the owls and the serpents—these serve as prophetic emblems of the future no less than of the past.

Byron was attracted by the seductive charm of ruins in a spirit of rumination and nostalgia for the past: he thinks of himself as 'a ruin amidst ruins'.[8] The stories he makes of these ruins are *myths*, in various senses. But we also hear in him a strong line of critical thought about the *history* embodied in those ruins, as an unfinished process into the future. Between these two attitudes there is a dynamic dialogue, played out in his writings, between myth (which is fixed) and history (which is not).

We can see this distinction between myth and history in a certain inconsistency in Byron's own attitude towards relics. Where the great Parthenon marbles were concerned, he was happy to denounce the depredations of his compatriots Lord Elgin and Lord Aberdeen. The latter, George Hamilton Gordon, fourth Earl of Aberdeen (1784–1860), was in fact his cousin. Though less notorious than Elgin, Aberdeen played a key role in shipping reliefs from the amphitheatre on the Pnyx in Athens back to London and securing the Parthenon marbles in 1806; he served as a Trustee of the British Museum and president of the Society of Antiquaries, before going on to a distinguished political career that culminated in terms as Foreign Secretary (1841–46) and Prime Minister (1852–55). Byron expressed his uninhibited scorn for them both in his early work, *English Bards and Scotch Reviewers* (1809):

---

8    *Childe Harold*, IV, 25; CPW II, 132. Amongst the many fine critical writings about the significance of 'ruins' and 'ruinology' for Byron and his contemporaries, see Clara Tuite, *Lord Byron and Scandalous Celebrity* (Cambridge: Cambridge University Press, 2015), especially her discussion of '*Childe Harold* IV and the pageant of his bleeding heart', pp. 139–67, where she argues for 'Byron's conjunction of the historical ruin poem and the melodrama of celebrity' (p. 144), and for the role of the poet's heart as both 'broken' and 'bleeding': 'Byron transforms the ruin genre by presenting the broken heart as a ruin and the experience of heartbreak through the topos of memory. The broken heart is a monument of ruin and the bleeding heart is corporeal, alive and present; the two figures intersect. [...] The poem joins topographical ruin affect with the affect of the broken heart, reverberating after lost love.' (p. 146)

> Let Aberdeen and Elgin still pursue
> The shade of fame through regions of Virtu;
> Waste useless thousands on their Phidian freaks,
> Mis-shapen monuments, and maimed antiques;
> And make their grand saloons a general mart
> For all the mutilated blocks of art:[9]

He displayed a similarly righteous indignation at Marathon, site of the famous battle between the Greeks and the Persians in 490 BCE. By contrast with the Parthenon, there was little remaining there to be seen, let alone purloined and shipped off. When the main funeral barrow was excavated, few or no relics were to be found. Instead, in the absence of any material signs of commemoration, the very plain of Marathon itself was offered to the poet for sale, he tells us, for a mere 'sixteen thousand piasters, about nine hundred pounds! Alas!', he exclaims, 'was the dust of Miltiades [the heroic Athenian general] worth no more? It could scarcely have fetched less if sold by *weight!*'[10]

Athens and Marathon carry—for Western readers—the aura of myth. But Byron could take a different view when the relics were less hallowed by myth than the sacred Athenian marbles or the tale of the battle of Marathon. The name of 'Morat' is far more deeply buried in history. In Canto III of *Childe Harold*, Byron writes about the bones of the Burgundian forces defeated at Morat by the Swiss in 1476, and in a note (to line 607) he confesses to having himself taken away some of these bones 'as much as may have made the quarter of a hero'.[11] Such humble human remains as these old bones lacked the charisma of those ancient Greek stories and artefacts; the very chapel that housed them had been destroyed. It is true that Byron aligns Morat and Marathon as sites where men fought for their liberty, in contrast to Waterloo and Cannae where states fought for dominion over each other (lines 608–9).[12] Yet the bones of those Burgundian soldiers are frail and exposed, both literally and figuratively. Byron's note betrays an anxiety about discriminating between theft and salvage, when he admits that his 'sole excuse is, that if I had not [taken the bones of the quarter of a hero], the next passer by

---

9    *English Bards and Scotch Reviewers*, lines 1027–32; CPW I, 261.
10   CPW II, 198.
11   CPW II, 307.
12   See McGann's commentary, CPW II, 307.

might have perverted them to worse uses than the careful preservation which I intend for them'.[13]

It comes as no surprise that Byron was the favourite poet of the American writer credited with uncovering the Maya ruins in Central America less than twenty years after Byron's death in 1824. Born in New Jersey, educated at Columbia College, and trained as a lawyer, John Lloyd Stephens (1805–52) set out for the 'Old World' in 1834, following Byron's footsteps. His first stop was Missolonghi in Greece, where Byron had famously died, fighting for Greek independence. In Odessa he narrowly avoided having his copy of Byron confiscated by Russian border-control.[14] He worked at high speed to publish two accounts of these travels: *Incidents of Travel in Egypt, Arabia Petræa, and the Holy Land* (1837), which went through six printings in its first year and sold some 21,000 copies, and then *Incidents of Travel in Greece, Turkey, Russia and Poland* (1838). The titles of all four of his books feature the word 'Incidents' with a purposive mock-modesty. Then in 1838, hungry for new adventures, Stephens turned his attention to Central America. He read Alexander von Humboldt's 1810 account of his Mexican visit, descriptions by Antonio del Rio and Guillermo Dupaix of the ruins of Palenque, and Juan Galindo's report of his 1835 expedition to Copán.[15] He teamed up with the English artist and architect Frederick Catherwood, who had also had extensive experience of the Old World territories and antiquities, and they set off together. They produced together in due course two best-selling publications, *Incidents of Travel in Central America, Chiapas and Yucatán* (1841), and *Incidents of Travel in Yucatán* (1843).[16]

---

13   *CPW* II, 307. McGann notes that Byron sent the bones back to his publisher John Murray in London, 'where they are still preserved'.

14   Byron was outlawed in Russia because of the scandalous portrayal of Catherine the Great in Cantos VI–X of *Don Juan* (1822). See Anya Taylor, 'Catherine the Great: Coleridge, Byron, and Erotic Politics on the Eastern Front', *Romanticism and Victorianism on the Net*, 61 (April 2012).

15   Karl Ackerman, introduction to new edition of J. L. Stephens's *Incidents of Travel in Central America, Chiapas, and Yucatán* (Washington and London: Smithsonian Institution Press, 1993), pp. 4–5.

16   Important too is Catherwood's independent volume of 1844, *Views of Ancient Monuments*, twenty-five hand-coloured lithographs, 300 copies, dedicated to Stephens. This was a scaled-down version of the more ambitious project for a huge volume (with Stephens) of 100–125 engravings, with texts by Prescott, Humboldt and others, which came to nothing. See Fabio Bourbon's modern edition, *The Lost*

Stephens's travel writings have attracted much interest over the last fifty years. Two dominant stories emerge. One portrays Stephens in a warm light, as a founding father of American archaeology, a heroic or at least admirable figure.[17] In the 1960s Donald Davie concluded his homage like this:

> And not that sort of hero, not
> Conquistador Aeneas, but a tourist!
> Uncoverer of the Maya, John L. Stephens,
> Blest after all those beaks and prows and horses.[18]

Well, not many tourists risk life and limb as fearlessly as Stephens and Catherwood. In fact it was exactly the risks the two of them ran that make the travel books such compelling reading: the sheer physical labour, the threat of violence and disease, everything from which the tourist industry seeks to protect its clients. Stephens might not be quite up to the epic feats of Stephen Spielberg's Indiana Jones but the movie legend owes something to the trail he blazed.[19] At a more august historical level, there are those for whom Stephens has more in common with the conquistador Aeneas or Cortez than with the tourists for whom he helped to pave the way.[20] In fact Stephens was writing only a few years before a traditional form of military intervention in the epoch-making war between the US and Mexico, following the American annexation of Texas in 1845. As for the great cultural artefacts he had 'uncovered',

---

*Cities of the Maya: The Life, Art and Discoveries of Frederick Catherwood* (Novara, Italy: De Agostini, 2014), and Victor W. Von Hagen, 'Artist of a Buried World', *American Heritage* 12.4 (June 1961).

17   See for example Victor W. Von Hagen, *Search for the Maya: the Story of Stephens and Catherwood* (London: Gordon and Cremonesi, 1978), and Larzer Ziff, *Return Passages: Great American Travel Writing, 1780–1910* (New Haven, CT and London: Yale University Press, 2000), pp. 58–117.

18   From 'Homage to John L. Stephens' (1964), *Collected Poems* (Manchester: Carcanet, 1990), p. 125.

19   Gesa Mackenthun, 'The Conquest of Antiquity: The Travelling Empire of John Lloyd Stephens', *American Travel and Empire*, ed. by Susan Castillo and David Seed (Liverpool: Liverpool University Press, 2009), p. 100.

20   Stephens was capable of fantasising about the business opportunities represented by a defunct volcano: 'I could not but reflect, what a waste of the bounties of Providence in this favoured but miserable land! At home this volcano would be a fortune; with a good hotel on top, a railing round to keep children from falling in, a zigzag staircase down the sides, and a glass of iced lemonade at the bottom.' (*Incidents of Travel in Central America*, II: 13).

Stephens felt few qualms about trying to buy them up and ship them off. The British Museum had the Parthenon marbles, so why couldn't 'we' do the equivalent?

There are two ways of appraising Stephens. He gets credit for recognising that the Maya ruins did not derive from the Old World, from the ancient Greeks or the Egyptians or the Israelites, but from an indigenous culture. On the other hand he promotes the myth of a single indigenous culture that *began* up north and gravitated south. And that therefore all its remains belong as of right to 'us. This confidence depends on a belief that 'we' Americans of the United States are, and will continue to be, as integrated an entity as 'those Central Americans' tearing each other apart in civil strife are not. Stephens did not foresee the Civil War that would rend the United States apart less than ten years after his death in 1852.

The political motives and consequences of Stephens's work may be clear (and 'conspicuous') to us now, but what role does his 'artistry' play? Are there no alternatives to the conquistador and the tourist? Do writers and artists simply collaborate with the politics of which they are servants? Or do they create a residue, a remnant of possibilities that could point in other directions? What of 'his [Stephens's] willingness to consider the monuments of Maya civilization in aesthetic, as well as merely historical or anthropological terms'? asks Nigel Leask. Perhaps this is 'his most enduring achievement, one which, uncommon in its own day, still challenges our contemporary post-colonial *episteme*'.[21] To this we should add the massive contribution of Catherwood's visual images.

Leask makes another helpful suggestion when he says that 'The books' archaeological interest is counterpointed, and often diluted, by its description of contemporary politics'.[22] David Brading says something similar, when he describes the contrast Stephens draws between 'ancient, forgotten, civilizations and contemporary political barbarism, the high aesthetic appeal of Maya sculpture undercut by

---

21    Nigel Leask, 'A Yankee in Yucatán: John Lloyd Stephens and the Lost Cities of America', in *Travel Writing in the Nineteenth Century: Filling the Blank Spaces*, ed. by Tim Youngs (London: Anthem Press 2012), p. 143.

22    Leask, 'A Yankee in Yucatán, p. 136.

the appalling civil wars of the present era'.[23] 'Diluted' and 'undercut': I would put it more strongly than this. The pressures of contemporary history to which Leask and Brading point are exactly what made the books so readable then and give them continuing value now.

Here I want to introduce a word that plays a significant role in Stephens's writing about the contemporary political situation in Central America: the word 'distracted' and the idea of 'distraction'. We normally now think of being distracted from something of greater importance to something of less, whether the importance is one of value or significance or risk or threat. Matthew Bevis rightly notes that the term 'appears to take on new life in twentieth-century society and culture', and that, as the antonym to 'attention', it has 'tended to get a bad press'.[24] It has certainly attracted much attention from writers and thinkers, from T. S. Eliot's memorable line in 'Burnt Norton' (1936) about being 'Distracted from distraction by distraction' to Saul Bellow's Oxford University lecture on 'The Distracted Public' (1990).[25] Bellow recognised the political implications of organised distraction and in recent years the word has acquired fresh currency as a way of describing political strategy.[26] However the only context in which we normally hear the word in its strongest sense is when we speak of being 'driven to distraction' or of being 'distraught'. To a modern ear the term usually implies something quite mild, unthreatening, whether a matter of irritation or pleasure, a 'diversion'.

When Byron writes of boating on Lake Leman, however, that 'This quiet sail is as a noiseless wing / To waft me from distraction',[27] he is thinking of 'distraction' as a state of violent disturbance, the turbulence of a world set on fire by the French Revolution and the consequent ruins,

---

23   Quoted by Leask, p. 136, from David Brading, *The First America, The Spanish Monarchy, Creole Patriots, and the Liberal State, 1492–1867* (Cambridge: Cambridge University Press, 1993), p. 629.

24   Though Bevis notes the 'bad press', his essay is primarily concerned with the creative potentialities of 'distraction', 'In Search of Distraction', *Poetry*, 211.2 (2017), 171–94 (176, 172).

25   'The Distracted Public', Romanes Lecture, Oxford University, 10 May 1990, in *It All Adds Up: From the Dim Past to the Uncertain Future* (London: Secker & Warburg, 1994), pp. 153–69.

26   E.g. 'Trump is a master of distraction and throwing out shiny objects to divert attention', writes David Smith, the *Guardian*, 25 Jan. 2019.

27   Canto III, 85; *CPW* II, 108.

and then the new dungeons and thrones that followed. The Latin roots of the word 'distraction' are about tearing or being torn apart. It is in this sense that Stephens repeatedly writes of the 'distracted state of the country' into which he ventures. It is the word he uses of Greece on his first arrival; it is the word he uses of Central America, a country 'distracted by a sanguinary civil war'; and it is the word he uses at the end of the Yucatán volume, as he laments the volcanic eruption of civil strife, again:

> Alas! before these pages were concluded, that country which we had looked upon as a picture of peace, and in which we had met with so much kindness, was torn and distracted by internal dissensions, the blast of civil war [...][28]

I have pointed to a contradiction in Byron's attitude towards the ruins of the ancient world. It was not a contradiction by which *he* was torn apart; on the contrary, it was for him a source of creative inspiration and power, a way of expressing his own doubts and uncertainties, a way of asking questions. For all the manifest differences between their literary projects, there is a comparable artistic motive at work in Stephens, a contradiction by which he was moved to write, and to which readers are invited to respond. On the one hand we recognise an indomitability, the sheer sense of physical risk, the determination to 'survive': from one perspective Stephens's writing is 'all about himself', though the self-characterisation is not triumphalist but self-deprecatory. Leask comments perceptively: 'In common with many post-romantic travel writers, Stephens often cultivates a self-parodic narrative voice to deal with this sense of belatedness, an attitude derived from his favourite poet Lord Byron.'[29] And on the other, there is at the heart of Stephens's adventure an interminable uncertainty about the history both past *and future* of the indigenous peoples with the ancient remains of whose artefacts he is 'dealing'.

Like Byron, Stephens was dismayed at the contrast between the greatness of the culture that produced these relics and the degradation of those living amidst them. Like Byron, he is sceptical about the

---

28   Stephens, *Incidents of Travel in Greece*, I, 7; *Incidents of Travel in Central America*, I, 3; *Incidents of Travel in Yucatán*, II, 455.
29   Leask, 'A Yankee in Yucatán', pp. 134–35.

possibilities of revival and renewal. Like Byron, he does not rule it out completely.[30] Like Byron, Stephens could not know what ruins, whether ancient or modern, portended for the future. But here the similarities break down before the massive difference between the ancient ruins over which Byron was meditating in Athens and Rome and those at which Stephens and Catherwood were staring, uncomprehendingly, in the Maya cities of Central America. Byron knew what his ruins meant, *or thought that he did*, because of all the stories that, for him and his readers, connected the past and the present.

Stephens too, in his travels round the 'Old World', sought and found connexions to shared collective memories. Throughout Greece and the Near East he encountered individuals who extended a welcome to the visitor from the 'New World'. In a convent on Mount Sinai, the Greek superior thanked him for the American support for his compatriots' struggle for independence. It had been the same everywhere, Stephens boasted: 'I remember a ploughman on immortal Marathon sang in my greedy ears the praises of America.'[31] Deep in the salt-mines of Wielitska in Poland, he could draw for making sense of them on 'Polish annals as early as twelve hundred and thirty-seven', on the legend of a prayer to St Anthony, the patron saint of Cracow.[32] From ancient Greece to medieval Poland, the stories abounded. But Central America was different. The Maya ruins at which Stephens and Catherwood stared were by contrast wholly illegible—and remained so until over a century after Catherwood copied all those glyphs so scrupulously.[33]

Ruins are not all about the past. They represent a past that once had a future—as we all do, a future that is by definition unknown. As witness the greatest of Romantic poems about ruins, 'Ozymandias' (1817), by Byron's friend Shelley, worth quoting here in full:

---

30 Towards the end of *Incidents of Travel in Yucatán*, he reflects that 'teaching might again lift up the Indian, might impart to him the skill to sculpture stone and carve wood; and if restored to freedom, and the unshackled exercise of his powers of mind, there might again appear a capacity to originate and construct, equal to that exhibited in the ruined monuments of his ancestors'. (II, 326)

31 Stephens, *Incidents of Travels in Egypt*, I, 277.

32 Stephens, *Incidents of Travels in Egypt*, I, 260–70.

33 See Michael D. Coe, *Breaking the Maya Code*, 3rd edn (London: Thames & Hudson, 2012).

I met a traveller from an antique land,
Who said—'Two vast and trunkless legs of stone
Stand in the desert . . . near them, on the sand,
Half sunk a shattered visage lies, whose frown,
And wrinkled lip, and sneer of cold command,
Tell that its sculptor well those passions read
Which yet survive, stamped on these lifeless things,
The hand that mocked them, and the heart that fed;
And on the pedestal, these words appear:
My name is Ozymandias, King of Kings;
Look on my Works, ye Mighty, and despair!
Nothing beside remains. Round the decay
Of that colossal Wreck, boundless and bare
The lone and level sands stretch far away'.—[34]

In 1847, Stephens finally met his great predecessor Alexander von Humboldt in Potsdam. Humboldt did not want to talk about the Maya ruins. He was much more interested in the war going on at that very moment between Mexico and the US.[35] War is a great distraction from archaeology, and vice-versa. Nothing makes ruins more swiftly than war—in Greece, in Yucatán, in Ukraine, wherever. As Byron knew.

But Byron could not have known the future that lay ahead for the ruins over which he lamented, in Athens and Rome. No more could Stephens and Catherwood as they contemplated the Maya ruins of Central America. The once sacred sites continue to be 'theatres of contention', to borrow Byron's significant phrase, again. How should we honour the past as it continues to occupy space—often precious if no longer sacred space?

In Britain we endure an interminable controversy about Stonehenge. The arguments are all about tourists and traffic, commerce, economy and logistics. How do we preserve these ancient monuments while catering for the pressing needs of the contemporary world, looking ahead to the future? There are so many interested parties: the ministry of defence, the farmers, the local inhabitants, the long-distance travellers,

---

34  *The Poems of Shelley*, vol. II, 1817–1819, ed. by Kelvin Everest and Geoffrey Matthews (Harlow: Longman, 2000), pp. 310–11.

35  Consider also the Caste War in Yucatán that broke out in 1847, five years after Stephens returned to New York, and would last for fifty years, as Leask points out: 'Stephens could never have guessed the train of events that were about to transform the region.' ('A Yankee in Yucatán', p. 139)

the tourists. 'Over the centuries this site has attracted as many theories about its construction as the Maya pyramids. It has been confidently credited to giants, wizards, Phoenicians, Mycenaeans, Romans, Saxons, Danes and aliens.' It has nothing like the grandeur of many other such ancient constructions, but it has played an extraordinarily powerful role in the collective imagination of 'Britishness'. 'Stonehenge, with the possible exception of Big Ben, is Britain's most recognisable monument. As a symbol of the nation's antiquity, it is our Parthenon, our pyramids—although, admittedly, less impressive.' The writer concludes that 'Stonehenge, then, is not so much about solidity and eternity as confusion and internal contradiction.'[36] Or in other words, about living history.

Meanwhile the great pyramid at the Maya ruins of Cobá in the northern Yucatán swarms with intrepid tourists.

Fig. 5.1 Adrian Poole and other tourists at Cobá, Mexico, November 2018. Photograph by Margaret de Vaux.

---

36   Charlotte Higgins, 'The Battle for the Future of Stonehenge', the *Guardian* Long Read, 8 February 2019. https://www.theguardian.com/uk-news/2019/feb/08/ the-battle-for-the-future-of-stonehenge
     See also, more recently, Steven Morris, 'Stonehenge campaigners' last-chance bid to save site from road tunnel', the *Guardian*, 11 December 2023. https://www.theguardian.com/uk-news/2023/dec/11/ stonehenge-campaigners-last-chance-bid-to-save-site-from-road-tunnel

Yet the site is not nearly as infested by the fairground ambience at the more commercially developed sites of Chichén Itzá and Tulúm, where the vendors endlessly tout Maya this and Maya that, including cheap hotel deals on the Maya Riviera. Not so different, after all, from the circus surrounding 'Old World' sites such as Mont St Michel, the Colosseum in Rome or the Acropolis in Athens. Or Stonehenge.

And yet of course the chaos of commerce and tourism is a world away from the violent mayhem that has surrounded, say, the ancient city of Palmyra, in the Syrian desert, north-east of Damascus.[37] Endlessly built and ruined, as it seems, only then to be restored and re-ruined. In August 2018 the web-site 'artnet' reported that 'Nearly Destroyed by ISIS, the Ancient City of Palmyra Will Reopen in 2019 After Extensive Renovations'.[38] What 'renovations' lie ahead, as I write in January 2024, for the cities of Ukraine and Gaza?

For ruins, there will always be a future.

---

37 In 1834 Catherwood travelled to Palmyra in native costume and made extensive drawings—which have not survived (Peter O. Koch, *John Lloyd Stephens and Frederick Catherwood: Pioneers of Mayan Archaeology* (Jefferson, NC and London: McFarland & Co., 2013), p. 42). A couple of years later Stephens's plans to go there fell through; he reported that 'the route to Palmyra is now entirely broken up by the atrocities of the Bedouins' (*Incidents of Travel in Egypt*, pp. 192, 193).

38 Sarah Cascone, 'Art World', *ArtNet*, 27 August 2018.
https://news.artnet.com/art-world/syria-isis-palmyra-restoration-1338257

# Bibliography

## Primary Sources

Byron, Lord G., *A Letter to * *** [John Murray] on the Rev. W. L. Bowles's Strictures on the Life and Writings of Pope* (London: John Murray, 1821).

Byron, Lord G., *Byron: The Complete Poetical Works*, ed. by Jerome J. McGann, 7 vols (Oxford: Clarendon Press, 1980–93).

Byron, Lord G., *Byron's Letters and Journals*, ed. by Leslie A. Marchand, 13 vols (London: John Murray, 1973–94).

Byron, Lord G., *Conversations of Lord Byron with the Countess of Blessington* (London: H. Colburn, 1834), https://babel.hathitrust.org/cgi/pt?id=dul1. ark:/13960/t2795c725&seq=13

Byron, Lord G., *English Bards, and Scotch Reviewers: a satire*, 2nd edn (London, 1809). Reprinted in https://petercochran.files.wordpress.com/2009/03/english-bards-and-scotch-reviewers1.pdf

Byron, Lord G., *Letters and Journals of Lord Byron: With Notices of His Life by Thomas Moore* (London: Murray, 1830).

[Byron, Lord G.], 'The Malediction of Minerva', *New Monthly Magazine* (April 1815).

## Secondary Sources

Ackerman, Karl, 'Introduction' in J. L. Stephens, *Incidents of Travel in Central America, Chiapas, and Yucatán* (Washington and London: Smithsonian Institution Press, 1993), pp. 4–5.

Andersen, H. C., *The True Story of My Life: A Sketch*, trans. by Mary Howitt (London: Longman, Brown, Green, and Longmans, 1847).

Anon., *Remarks on the Exclusion of Lord Byron's Monument from Westminster Abbey*, n.d. [London, 1844].

Barnard, M. R., *The Life of Thorvaldsen, Collated from the Danish of J. M. Thiele* (London: Chapman and Hall, 1865).

Bartholdy, J. L. S., *Voyage en Grèce* (Paris: Dentu, 1807), https://www.google.co.uk/books/edition/Voyage_en_Gr%C3%A8ce_1803_04/TZ8wAAAAYAAJ?hl=en&gbpv=1

Beevers, Robert, 'Pretensions to Permanency: Thorvaldsen's Bust and Statue of Byron', *The Byron Journal*, 23 (1995), 63–75.

Black, William, *Narratives of Cruises in the Mediterranean* (Edinburgh: Oliver and Boyd, 1900), https://wellcomecollection.org/works/b69gt278/items

Bond, Geoffrey and Christine Kenyon Jones, *Dangerous to Show: Byron and His Portraits* (London: Unicorn, 2020).

Bourbon, Fabio, *The Lost Cities of the Maya: The Life, Art and Discoveries of Frederick Catherwood* (Novara, Italy: De Agostini, 2014).

Brading, David, *The First America, The Spanish Monarchy, Creole Patriots, and the Liberal State, 1492–1867* (Cambridge: Cambridge University Press, 1993).

Broughton, Lord [John Cam Hobhouse], *Recollections of a Long Life*, 6 vols (London: John Murray, 1909–11), https://archive.org/details/recollectionsofa007946mbp

Buzard, James, *The Beaten Track: European Tourism, Literature, and the Ways to 'Culture', 1800–1918* (Oxford: Clarendon Press, 1993).

Cascone, Sarah, 'Art World', *ArtNet*, 27 August 2018, https://news.artnet.com/art-world/syria-isis-palmyra-restoration-1338257

Clark, J. W., *Cambridge, Historical and Descriptive Notes* (London: Seeley & Co., 1890).

Clarke, Edward Daniel, *Travels in Various Countries of Europe, Asia and Africa*, 6 vols (London: Printed for T. Cadell and W. Davies, 1810–23), https://wellcomecollection.org/works/ddmjahws/items

Clogg, Richard, ed. and trans., *The Movement for Greek Independence, 1770–1821* (London: Macmillan, 1976).

Cochran, Peter, *Byron and Hobby-O: Lord Byron's Relationship with John Cam Hobhouse* (Newcastle-upon-Tyne: Cambridge Scholars Publishing, 2010).

Coe, Michael D., *Breaking the Maya Code*, 3rd edn (London: Thames & Hudson, 2012).

Comte de Forbin, Louis, *Voyage dans le Levant en 1817 et 1818*, 2 vols, 2nd edn (Paris: Delaunay, 1819), https://www.google.co.uk/books/edition/Voyage_dans_le_Levant_en_1817_et_1818/cFY9AAAAcAAJ?hl=en&gbpv=1&printsec=frontcover

Dodwell, Edward, *A Classical and Topographical Tour through Greece, during the years 1801, 1805, and 1806*, 2 vols (London: Rodwell and Martin, 1819), https://www.

google.co.uk/books/edition/A_Classical_and_Topographical_Tour_Throu/sgkXAAAAYAAJ?hl=en&gbpv=1

Douglas, F. S. N., *An Essay on Certain Points of Resemblance between the Ancient and Modern Greeks* (London: John Murray, 1813), https://archive.org/details/anessayoncertai00dougoog

Elfenbein, Andrew, *Byron and the Victorians* (Cambridge: Cambridge University Press, 1995).

Eliot, C. W. J., 'Lord Byron, Early Travelers, and the Monastery at Delphi', *American Journal of Archaeology*, 71 (1967), 283–91.

Eliot, T. S., *The Complete Prose of T. S. Eliot: The Critical Edition, Volume 5: Tradition and Orthodoxy, 1934–1939*, ed. by Iman, Javadi, Ronald Schuchard and Jayme Stayer (Baltimore, MA, and London: The Johns Hopkins University Press and Faber & Faber Ltd., 2017). https://doi.org/10.1353/book.67878

Erdman, David V. and David Worrall, eds., *Manuscripts of the Younger Romantics VI: Childe Harold's Pilgrimage* (New York: Garland 1991).

Eustace, J. C., *A Tour through Italy*, 2 vols (London: J. Mawman, 1813), https://archive.org/details/classicaltouritaly03eust

Everest, Kelvin and Geoffrey Matthews, eds., *The Poems of Shelley*, vol. II, 1817–1819 (Harlow: Longman, 2000).

François-René, vicomte de Chateaubriand, *Travels to Jerusalem and the Holy Land, through Egypt*, 2 vols, 3rd edn, trans. by Frederic Shoberl (London: H. Colburn, 1835), https://archive.org/details/travelstojerusal02chat/page/n5/mode/2up

Galt, John, *Autobiography* (London: Cochrane and M'Crone, 1833).

Galt, John, *Letters from the Levant* (London: T. Cadell and W. Davies, 1813), https://www.google.co.uk/books/edition/Letters_from_the_Levant/7A4IAAAAQAAJ?hl=en&gbpv=1

Galt, John, *Life of Byron* (London: Henry Colburn and Richard Bentley, 1830), https://www.google.co.uk/books/edition/The_Life_of_Lord_Byron/guwyAQAAMAAJ?hl=en&gbpv=1

Haygarth, William, *Greece, A Poem in Three Parts* (London: W. Bulmer & Co, 1814), https://www.google.co.uk/books/edition/Greece/_oJOAQAAMAAJ?hl=en&gbpv=1

Higgins, Charlotte, 'The Battle for the Future of Stonehenge', *The Guardian*, 8 February 2019, https://www.theguardian.com/uk-news/2019/feb/08/the-battle-for-the-future-of-stonehenge

Hobhouse, John Cam, *A Journey through Albania and other provinces of Turkey in Europe and Asia, to Constantinople, during the years 1809 and 1810* (London: James Cawthorne, 1813), https://www.google.co.uk/books/edition/A_Journey_Through_Albania_and_Other_Prov/8nfVAAAAMAAJ?hl=en&gbpv=1

Hobhouse, John Cam, Letter to John Murray, 31 Aug 1829 (John Murray Archive).

Hodgson, James T., *Memoir of the Rev. Francis Hodgson, B.D., scholar, poet, and divine: with numerous letters from Lord Byron and others, by his son, James T. Hodgson*, 2 vols (London: Macmillan, 1878), https://www.digitale-sammlungen.de/en/view/bsb11370276?page=346,347

Hogg, Thomas Jefferson, *The Life of Percy Bysshe Shelley*, 2 vols (London: Edward Moxon, 1858), https://www.google.co.uk/books/edition/The_Life_of_Percy_Bysshe_Shelley/O18JAAAAQAAJ?hl=en&gbpv=1

Honour, Hugh, *Neoclassicism* (Harmondsworth: Penguin, 1968).

Hughes, T. S., *Travels in Sicily, Greece and Albania*, 2 vols (London: J. Mawman, 1820), https://archive.org/details/travelsinsicily01hughgoog/page/n5/mode/2up

Jones, George, R.A., *Sir Francis Chantrey, R.A.: Recollections of his Life, Practice, and Opinions* (London: E. Moxon, 1849), https://archive.org/details/sirfrancischantr00joneiala

Keach, William, 'Romantic Writing and the Determinations of Cultural Property', *European Romantic Review*, 30 (2019), 223–37, https://doi.org/10.1080/10509585.2019.1612586

Koch, Peter O., *John Lloyd Stephens and Frederick Catherwood: Pioneers of Mayan Archaeology* (Jefferson, NC and London: McFarland & Co., 2013).

Leask, Nigel, 'A Yankee in Yucatán: John Lloyd Stephens and the Lost Cities of America', in *Travel Writing in the Nineteenth Century: Filling the Blank Spaces*, ed. by Tim Youngs (London: Anthem Press 2012), https://doi.org/10.7135/UPO9781843317692.008

Lockhart, J. G., *The Life of Sir Walter Scott, Bart*, one-volume edition (London: Adam & Charles Black, 1893).

Mackenthun, Gesa, 'The Conquest of Antiquity: The Travelling Empire of John Lloyd Stephens' in *American Travel and Empire*, ed. by Susan Castillo and David Seed (Liverpool: Liverpool University Press, 2009), https://doi.org/10.5949/liverpool/9781846311802.003.0006

Marchand, Leslie A., *Byron: A Biography*, 3 vols (London: John Murray, 1957).

Michaelis, Adolf, *Ancient Marbles in Great Britain*, trans. by C. A. M. Fennell (Cambridge: Cambridge University Press, 1882), https://archive.org/details/ancientmarblesin00michuoft

Morris, Steven, 'Stonehenge campaigners' last-chance bid to save site from road tunnel', *The Guardian*, 11 December 2023. https://www.theguardian.com/uk-news/2023/dec/11/stonehenge-campaigners-last-chance-bid-to-save-site-from-road-tunnel

Oliphant, Mrs, *Annals of a Publishing House: William Blackwood and his sons, their magazine and friends*, 2 vols (Edinburgh and London: Blackwood, 1897–98).

Parker Willis, N., *Summer Cruise in the Mediterranean* (London: T. Nelson and Sons, 1853), https://www.gutenberg.org/ebooks/48264

Plon, Eugène, *Thorvaldsen: His Life and Works*, trans. by Mrs Cashel Hoey (London: Richard Bentley, 1874).

Poole, Adrian, 'Byron in Yucatán: War and Ruins', published in *The Influence and Legacy of Alexander von Humboldt in the Americas*, ed. by María Fernanda Valencia Suarez and Carolina Depetris (Mérida: Universidad Nacional Autónoma de México, 2022), pp. 119–31.

Pope, Willard Bissell, ed., *The Diary of Benjamin Robert Haydon* 5 vols (Cambridge, MA: Harvard University Press, 1963).

Pouqueville, F. C. H. L., *Voyage dans la Grèce*, 5 vols (Paris: Firmin Didot, Père et Fils, 1820–21), https://gallica.bnf.fr/ark:/12148/bpt6k97401533.image

Praz, Mario, *On Neo-Classicism* (London: Thames and Hudson, 1969).

Robson-Scott, W. D., *The Younger Goethe and the Visual Arts* (Cambridge: Cambridge University Press, 1981).

Robson, Robert, 'Byron's Rooms Revisited', *The Trinity Review* (Easter 1975), 22–24.

Sass, Else K., 'The Classical Tradition in Later European Portraiture, with Special Regard to Thorvaldsen's Portraits', *Proceedings of the Second International Congress of Classical Studies*, vol. III: *The Classical Pattern of Modern Western Civilization, Portraiture* (Copenhagen: E. Munksgaard, 1957).

Sinker, Robert, 'The Statue of Byron in the Library of Trinity College, Cambridge', *Notes and Queries*, 6.4 (December 1881), 421–28, https://babel.hathitrust.org/cgi/pt?id=mdp.39015020441013&seq=612

Smith, A. H., 'Lord Elgin and His Collection', *The Journal of Hellenic Studies*, 36 (1916), 163–372.

[Smith, James and Horatio Smith], *Horace in London* (London: John Miller, 1813).

Spence, Joseph, *Anecdotes, Observations and Characters, of Books and Men* (Cambridge: Cambridge University Press, 1820).

Spencer, Terence, *Fair Greece, Sad Relic: Literary Philhellenism from Shakespeare to Byron* (London: Weidenfeld & Nicholson, 1954).

St Clair, William, 'The Impact of Byron's Writings: An Evaluative Approach', in *Byron, Augustan and Romantic*, ed. by Andrew Rutherford (Basingstoke: Macmillan, 1990), pp. 1–25.

St Clair, William, *Lord Elgin and the Marbles: The Controversial History of the Parthenon Sculptures*, 3rd rev edn (Oxford and New York: Oxford University Press, 1998).

St Clair, William, *That Greece Might Still Be Free: The Philhellenes in the War of Independence*, new edition (Cambridge: Open Book Publishers, 2008), https://doi.org/10.11647/OBP.0001

Taylor, Anya, 'Catherine the Great: Coleridge, Byron, and Erotic Politics on the Eastern Front', *Romanticism and Victorianism on the Net*, 61 (April 2012) https://doi.org/10.7202/1018597ar

Thiele, J. M., *Thorvaldsen in Rome, 1805–1819*, 4 vols (Copenhagen, 1852).

Thorvaldsen, Bertel, Letter from Bertel Thorvaldsen to John Cam Hobhouse, 25 July 1829 (from a transcription of the original in the John Murray Archive).

Tournikiotis, Panayotis, ed., *The Parthenon and its Impact in Modern Times* (Athens: Melissa, 1994).

Tsigakou, Fani-Maria, *The Rediscovery of Greece: Travellers and Romantics in the Nineteenth Century* (London: Fine Art Society, 1979).

Tsigakou, Fani-Maria, *Through Romantic Eyes: European images of nineteenth-century Greece from the Benaki Museum, Athens* (Athens, 1991).

Tuite, Clara, *Lord Byron and Scandalous Celebrity* (Cambridge: Cambridge University Press, 2015) https://doi.org/10.1017/CBO9781316009666

Turner, William, *Journal of a Tour in the Levant*, 3 vols (London: John Murray, 1820); vol. I, https://www.google.co.uk/books/edition/Journal_of_a_Tour_in_the_Levant/dCoNAAAAYAAJ?hl=en&gbpv=1

Von Hagen, Victor W., 'Artist of a Buried World', *American Heritage*, 12.4 (June 1961).

Von Hagen, Victor W., *Search for the Maya: The Story of Stephens and Catherwood* (London: Gordon and Cremonesi, 1978).

Wanscher, Wilhelm, *Artes*, tome 1 (Copenhagen, 1932).

Winckelmann, Johann Joachim, *Winckelmann: Writings on Art*, selected and ed. by David Irwin (London: Phaidon, 1972).

Wise, Thomas James, *A Bibliography of the Writings in Verse and Prose of George Gordon, Lord Byron* (London: private circulation, 1933). Repr. edn (Folkestone, Kent: Dawsons of Pall Mall), https://archive.org/details/bibliographyofwr0002wise_t1q8/page/n5/mode/2up.

Woodhouse, C. M., *Capodistria: The Founder of Greek Independence* (New York: Oxford University Press, 1973).

Wordsworth, William, *The Prelude* (London: Moxon, 1850).

Wright, M. F., *Alma Mater, or Seven Years at the University of Cambridge, by a Trinity-Man* (London: Black and Young, 1827).

Ziff, Larzer, *Return Passages: Great American Travel Writing, 1780–1910* (New Haven, CT and London: Yale University Press, 2000).

# Index

# About the Team

Alessandra Tosi was the managing editor for this book.

Jennifer Moriarty proofread this manuscript, indexed it, and created the Alt-text.

Tricia De Souza and Rose Cook provided editorial assistance.

Jeevanjot Kaur Nagpal designed the cover. The cover was produced in InDesign using the Fontin font.

Cameron Craig typeset the book in InDesign and produced the paperback and hardback editions. The text font is Tex Gyre Pagella and the heading font is Californian FB.

Jeremy Bowman produced the EPUB edition.

Cameron produced the PDF, and HTML editions. The conversion was performed with open-source software and other tools freely available on our GitHub page at https://github.com/OpenBookPublishers.

# This book need not end here...

## Share

All our books — including the one you have just read — are free to access online so that students, researchers and members of the public who can't afford a printed edition will have access to the same ideas. This title will be accessed online by hundreds of readers each month across the globe: why not share the link so that someone you know is one of them?

This book and additional content is available at:
https://doi.org/10.11647/OBP.0399

## Donate

Open Book Publishers is an award-winning, scholar-led, not-for-profit press making knowledge freely available one book at a time. We don't charge authors to publish with us: instead, our work is supported by our library members and by donations from people who believe that research shouldn't be locked behind paywalls.

Why not join them in freeing knowledge by supporting us:
https://www.openbookpublishers.com/support-us

Follow @OpenBookPublish

Read more at the Open Book Publishers BLOG

# You may also be interested in:

## That Greece Might Still Be Free
### The Philhellenes in the War of Independence
*William St Clair*

https://doi.org/10.11647/obp.0001

## Romanticism and Time
### Literary Temporalities
*Sophie Laniel-Musitelli and Céline Sabiron (editors)*

https://doi.org/10.11647/obp.0232

## An Outline of Romanticism in the West
*John Claiborne Isbell*

https://doi.org/10.11647/obp.0302

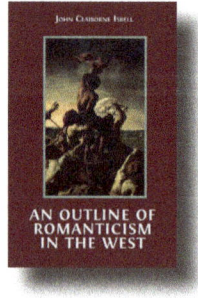

Milton Keynes UK
Ingram Content Group UK Ltd.
UKHW050057290424
441884UK00001B/1